Collins

AQA GCSE 9-1
English Language
& Literature

Workbook

Paul Burns

Preparing for the GCSE Exam

Revision That Really Works

Experts have found that there are two techniques that help you to retain and recall information and consistently produce better results in exams compared to other revision techniques.

It really isn't rocket science either – you simply need to:

- **test yourself** on each topic as many times as possible
- **leave a gap** between the test sessions.

Three Essential Revision Tips

1. **Use Your Time Wisely**
   - Allow yourself plenty of time.
   - Try to start revising at least six months before your exams – it's more effective and less stressful.
   - Don't waste time re-reading the same information over and over again – it's not effective!

2. **Make a Plan**
   - Identify all the topics you need to revise.
   - Plan at least five sessions for each topic.
   - One hour should be ample time to test yourself on the key ideas for a topic.
   - Spread out the practice sessions for each topic – the optimum time to leave between each session is about one month but, if this isn't possible, just make the gaps as big as realistically possible.

3. **Test Yourself**
   - Methods for testing yourself include: quizzes, practice questions, flashcards, past papers, explaining a topic to someone else, etc.
   - Don't worry if you get an answer wrong – provided you check what the correct answer is, you are more likely to get the same or similar questions right in future!

Visit **collins.co.uk/collinsGCSErevision** for more information about the benefits of these techniques, and for further guidance on how to plan ahead and make them work for you.

Command Words Used in Exam Questions

This table shows the meanings of some of the most commonly used command words in GCSE exam questions.

Command word	Meaning
List…	Pick out words or phrases and copy them. Do not comment on them.
Choose…	Pick the correct statements and fill in the box.
Look in detail…	Carefully re-read the appropriate part of the text before giving a detailed answer.
Focus on…	Your answer should be about the section of text indicated and not about the rest of the source.
How…?	Write about the writer's methods, e.g. use of language and structure.
How far…?/To what extent…?	You are free to agree, disagree or partly agree. Answer the question in detail using appropriate references.
Describe/Write a description…	Describe something; do NOT write a story.
Refer to both…	Write equally about both sources.
Explore/Explain…	Write a detailed answer using appropriate references and terminology.
Starting with the extract, explore/explain…	About half your answer should be a detailed analysis of the extract you are given.
Compare…	Write equally about the two texts, focusing on their similarities and differences.

Contents

Key Technical Skills: Writing

Spelling

Grade 2-3

1 Insert the correctly spelled word in each of the following pairs of sentences:

a) your/you're

Is that _____ coat?

_____ in the wrong place.

b) there/ they're/ their

_____ all in the yard eating

_____ lunches, over

_____ by the tree.

c) where/ wear/ were

What do you think I should

_____ for the party?

_____ did you say they

_____ going?

d) hear/here

Come over _____. I can't

_____ you very well.

e) to/ too/ two

You have _____ choose

_____ of the five

options. Three would be

_____ many.

f) its/it's

The cat's eaten _____ food

and now _____

asleep.   [15]

Grade 3-5

2 The following passage contains ten incorrect spellings. Underline them and then write the correct spellings below.

If you are going to improve your preformance in any area, weather in a sport, a hobby or in you're studys, you must practice. Succesfull people who have acheived great things in life always say it is becos of hard work just as much as talent. You mite not want to be an Olympic champion, but you can still get a lot of satisfaction from nowing you have improved.

_____

_____

_____

_____ [10]

Grade 4-6

3 Put the following words into their plural forms:

a) tornado _____

b) woman _____

c) antibody _____

d) antithesis _____

e) soliloquy _____ [5]

GCSE English Workbook

Total Marks = _____ / 30

Key Technical Skills: Writing

Punctuation

Grade 2–3

1 Punctuate the following passage using only full stops and insert a capital letter after each one. There should be five full stops.

Anita and Me is a novel based on the author's own childhood it is the story of a family who come from India they settle in a village in the English Midlands the narrator makes friends with a girl called Anita their friendship is the focus of the book

_____

_____

_____ [5]

Grade 4–6

2 Add five commas and five apostrophes to the passage below.

Pride and Prejudice is Jane Austens most popular book. Elizabeth one of five sisters meets a man called Mr Darcy who is very rich and rather snobbish. Darcys best friend whose name is Mr Bingley falls in love with Elizabeths older sister. The sisters relationships dont go smoothly.

_____

_____

_____ [10]

Grade 5+

3 Add a question mark, an exclamation mark, a colon, a semi-colon or brackets to the following pairs of clauses so that they make sense.

a) Where did they come from nobody knows.

_____

b) What a lovely surprise it was just what I wanted.

_____

c) Pip the hero of the story meets Magwitch on the marshes.

_____

d) Kai had rice pudding Ellie chose the cheese.

_____

e) We love Birmingham it has everything a city should have.

_____ [5]

Total Marks = _____ / 20

Key Technical Skills: Writing

Sentence Structure

Grade 1–3

1 Combine the following simple sentences to form compound sentences using the conjunctions **and** or **but**.

a) Jo lives next door to me. Mo lives next door to her.

_____

b) Mo has a dog. Jo does not have any pets.

_____   **[2]**

Grade 3–5

2 Combine the following simple sentences to form complex sentences using the conjunctions **because** or **although**.

a) He worked as quickly as he could. He did not finish on time.

_____

b) I missed the bus. I stopped to talk to someone on the way.

_____   **[2]**

Grade 3–5

3 Combine the following sentences to form a complex sentence using a relative pronoun.

Tom is my best friend. He lives on the main road.

_____   **[1]**

Grade 5+

4 Identify whether the sentences below are simple, complex, compound or minor sentences.

a) Bella jumped for joy. _____

b) Nana cut the cake and everyone sang 'Happy Birthday'. _____

c) Brilliant! _____

d) Trying my best to be cheerful, despite my misgivings, I joined in with

the celebrations. _____

e) Do not leave this room until you have tidied up. _____   **[5]**

Total Marks = _____ / 10

Key Technical Skills: Writing

> ## Text Structure and Organisation

1 Rearrange the following paragraphs so that the passage makes sense. Put the paragraphs in the correct order.

a) These groups have achieved a lot but their efforts have had little impact on the behaviour of people passing through on their way to the shops and bars on the main road. ☐

b) The residents of Manningham Drive say they have had enough of noise, litter and generally anti-social behaviour in their neighbourhood. ☐

c) We asked both the council and the police for their response to Ms Braithwaite's comments but, so far, they have not replied. ☐

d) They have had a number of meetings and have organised an army of volunteers to deal with the litter and graffiti problem. They go out regularly in groups every week to pick up rubbish and clean up. ☐

e) Spokesperson Lizzie Braithwaite said, 'We are doing everything we can to improve our neighbourhood but we can only do so much. We are calling on the police and the local council to deal with anti-social behaviour in the street. So far they have done nothing.' ☐ **[5]**

2 Insert each of these five discourse markers or connectives into the passage so that it makes sense:

| nevertheless | after | therefore | despite | however |

a) _____ I got your letter, I decided to visit Manningham Drive.

b) _____ serving as your councillor for six months, I am sorry to say that I

was unaware of the extent of the problem. Thanks to your group, **c)** _____,

I now appreciate how the residents feel. I have, **d)** _____, contacted

the appropriate council department and the Chief Constable. They have not yet replied.

e) _____, I shall continue to pursue the matter on your behalf. **[5]**

> Total Marks = _____ / 10

Key Technical Skills: Writing

Standard English and Grammar

Grade 3–6

1 In the following sentences, insert the correct form of the verb 'to be' or 'to do'.

Present tense

a) You _____ taller than me.

b) They _____ brothers.

Simple past tense

c) We _____ the first to arrive.

d) She _____ all her homework.

Perfect tense

e) He _____ in my class for three years.

f) They _____ all the cooking for the party.

Simple past + Past perfect

g) We _____ pleased with the result because

we _____ everything asked of us.   **[8]**

Grade 4–6

2 Which of the following is correct in Standard English? Circle the correct words.

a) They have **got/gotten** their **invites/invitations** to the party.

b) He's one of the **only/few** people to have **broke/broken** the sound barrier.   **[4]**

Grade 5+

3 Rewrite the following passage using Standard English.

I was stood in the street minding me own business when I seen Zaki. He come over to me acting dead casual. Me and Zaki was best mates. I was gonna ask him how he done in his exams. I never said nothing though. I could see he done good. Then I clocked Kirsty sat on the wall. 'Did you guys flunk your exams again?' she shouted.

_____

_____

_____

_____

_____

_____   **[8]**

Total Marks = _____ / 20

Key Technical Skills: Reading

Explicit Information and Ideas

1 Read the passage below.

> The Muncaster family has been farming on Windle Top for over a hundred years. In their dairy farm they have over 150 cattle. In the summer, the cattle stay out in the fields and are brought in for milking twice a day. Gerry and Annie Muncaster say it's a hard life but very rewarding. They hope that their children will follow them into farming one day.

Which of the statements below contain information that is explicitly stated in the text? Tick the correct answers.

a) The Muncasters are farmers. ☐

b) Gerry inherited the farm from his father. ☐

c) There are over 150 cattle on the farm. ☐

d) Gerry and Annie do not enjoy farming. ☐

e) The cattle are milked twice a day. ☐

f) The Muncasters have a lot of children. ☐

g) Windle Top is in Yorkshire. ☐

h) According to the Muncasters, farming is a rewarding job. ☐ [4]

2 Read the passage below.

> He was a very nice looking old gentleman, and he looked as if he were nice, too, which is not at all the same thing. He had a fresh-coloured, clean-shaven face, and white hair, and he wore rather odd-shaped collars and a top hat that wasn't exactly the same kind as other people's.
>
> From *The Railway Children* by E. Nesbit

List four things that we learn about the old gentleman's appearance.

_____

_____

_____

_____ [4]

Total Marks = _____ / 8

Key Technical Skills: Reading

Implicit Information and Ideas

Grade 3–4

1 Which of the following statements...

A imply that the writer enjoys living on a farm?
B imply that the writer does not enjoy living on a farm?
C give no indication of the writer's feelings.

Write the appropriate letter in the boxes.

a) I know one thing. I will never set foot on a farm again. ☐

b) There's something special about working with animals and growing crops. ☐

c) We grow wheat, barley and corn on the farm. ☐

d) My sister hates farming. ☐

e) I miss shopping, nights out in town, my family and my friends. ☐

f) I was a real townie and it took a while, but I'm really glad I moved here. ☐

g) It is three miles from the farm to the nearest village. ☐

h) Every night on the farm I go to bed feeling that I've achieved something worthwhile. ☐ [8]

Grade 3–4

2 Read the following passage.

The narrator has just seen some Martians that have arrived on Earth.

> I turned and, running madly, made for the first group of trees, perhaps a hundred yards away; but I ran slantingly and stumblingly, for I could not avert my eyes from these things.
>
> From *The War of the Worlds* by HG Wells.

Which of the following statements are TRUE? Tick the statements that are implied by what the narrator says.

a) The narrator is frightened. ☐

b) The narrator has never seen a Martian before. ☐

c) The narrator is old. ☐

d) The narrator thinks the Martians are friendly. ☐

e) The narrator is fascinated by the Martians. ☐

f) The narrator is a Martian. ☐

g) The narrator thinks he will be safer amongst the trees. ☐

h) The narrator runs very fast. ☐ [4]

Total Marks = _____ / 12

Synthesis and Summary 1

1 Reduce each of the following sentences to five words by crossing out, in order to give the necessary information without losing sense.

a) Jackie, who has long dark hair, won the sack race.

b) I must insist that you give me the letter now.

c) A vengeful wind blew over the two much-loved trees. [3]

2 Read the following statement from someone who has witnessed an accident.

> I spent most of the day at my nan's house, number 5 Roland Street. I love going there because she always spoils me with sweets and presents. When I left at four o'clock, it was very windy. It was cold as well but I was well wrapped up so it didn't bother me. When I was at the front gate, I saw a car coming round the corner from Bilton Road. Just as it turned, a tree in the garden of the corner house was blown right over and landed across the car's bonnet. The driver braked suddenly. I ran over to see if anyone was hurt. As I approached, I could see two people inside, though my view wasn't clear because of the tree being in the way. By the time I got there they were getting out of the car. They must have had a terrible shock, but they seemed okay. Nan came down the street then and so did a few of the neighbours. It's a very close community.

If you were investigating the accident, which **five** of the following pieces of information would be most relevant to understanding what had happened? Tick the correct answers.

a) The witness was in Roland Street at four o'clock. ☐

b) The witness's nan spoils them with sweets and presents. ☐

c) The witness was dressed for cold and windy weather. ☐

d) The car came round the corner from Bilton Road. ☐

e) The wind blew over a tree in the garden of the corner house. ☐

f) The tree landed across the car's bonnet. ☐

g) The witness thinks the people in the car must have had a shock. ☐

h) Two people got out of the car and appeared unhurt. ☐

i) People came out of their houses. ☐

j) People in Roland Street are very friendly. ☐ [5]

3 On a separate piece of paper, write a summary of the witness's statement. Aim for 50 words or fewer. [12]

Total Marks = _____ / 20

Key Technical Skills: Reading

Synthesis and Summary 2

Grade 3–5

1 Read the two passages below.

A This text is adapted from a letter written by 'JDS' to *The Liverpool Mercury* in 1832. A turnpike road was a private road which people had to pay tolls to use.

> GENTLEMEN, I should feel particularly obliged to you or any of your readers if you could inform me by whose authority the turnpike on the Aigburth road was established, and why the public at large are required to pay tolls there when the inhabitants of that neighbourhood are exempted. I think it not only a nuisance, but a complete imposition, which calls loudly for inquiry. I have heard, a few interested individuals round there had in a former period been at an expense (mark, for their own convenience) in repairing the road, but it has long since paid itself over and over again; and, let me ask, who pockets the money collected there now? The road is kept in excellent repair for about one-quarter of a mile beyond the gate, but on approaching Garston it is very bad.

B This is an email sent to a local council about the roads near the writer, Amina's, home.

> Hi, I really am getting fed up with this now. I've written umpteen emails and texts to you about the state of the High Street. There are two main problems: parking and that road surface. There are double yellow lines along a fair proportion of the road. Why do so many people ignore them or, worse still, think it's okay to park either half-on and half-off the pavement or even entirely on the pavement, creating an obstacle course for prams and wheelchairs? This is against the law. And as for the road surface… it's pothole city outside my shop. I've lived and worked here for ten years; every year it gets worse and nobody does anything about it. What are we paying our council tax and business rates for?

Pick out as many similarities and differences as you can between the contents of the two sources. Write them in the table below or on a separate piece of paper. There may be more differences than similarities. Do not comment on language or style.

Similarities	Differences

[10]

Grade 4–6+

2 Now sum up the similarities and differences in the texts above, writing in proper sentences. Do not comment on language or style. Continue on a separate piece of paper.

_____

_____

_____

_____

[8]

Total Marks = _____ / 18

Key Technical Skills: Reading

Referring to the Text

Grade 1–3

1 Match each statement **a)–c)** with its paraphrase **x)–z)**:

a) I was proceeding towards the location from which the sound emanated.

b) I am anxious to ascertain the identity of the perpetrator.

c) At 21.30 we took our leave of the apartment which was our home.

x) At half past nine we left our flat.

y) I was going to the place the noise came from.

z) I want to find out who did it.

_____ [3]

Grade 3–5

2 The following sentences all include quotations from *Romeo and Juliet*, which have not been set out correctly. Set them out correctly using colons and/or quotation marks where appropriate.

a) Romeo refers to Juliet as a bright angel. _____

_____

_____

b) Romeo rejects his family Henceforth I never will be Romeo. _____

_____

_____

c) When Juliet asks how he found her, Romeo replies By love, that first did prompt me to enquire. He lent me counsel, and I lent him eyes. _____

_____

_____ [6]

Grade 3–5

3 Here are two examples of the use of PEE. Use different colours to highlight the point, the evidence and the explanation (or exploration).

a) Gratiano insults Shylock, calling him 'an inexecrable dog', a metaphor that implies that he considers Shylock less than human.

b) By the end of the novel, Scrooge is a reformed character, shown by his gift of the turkey to the Cratchits, a generous gesture that the old Scrooge would never have made. [6]

Total Marks = _____ / 15

Key Technical Skills: Reading

Analysing Language 1

Grade 2–3

1 Read the passage below and identify the word class (part of speech) of the bold words.

> Apparently, the vegetable **kingdom** in Mars, instead of having green for a **dominant** colour, is of a vivid blood-red tint. At any rate, **the** seeds which the Martians (intentionally **or accidentally**) **brought with them** gave rise in all cases to red-coloured growths.
>
> From *The War of the Worlds* by HG Wells

Choose from: **pronoun adjective verb adverb noun conjunction determiner preposition**

a) kingdom _____

b) dominant _____

c) the _____

d) or _____

e) accidentally _____

f) brought _____

g) with _____

h) them _____   [8]

Grade 2–3

2 a) Give an example from the passage of a proper noun. _____

b) There are two sentences in the passage above. What sort of sentence are they?

_____

c) Give an example of a relative pronoun from the passage. _____

d) Are the sentences in the active or passive voice? _____   [4]

Grade 4–6

3 a) Which two of these terms could be used to describe the register of the passage above?

formal   colloquial   technical   dialectical

_____ and _____   [2]

b) Explain why you have chosen these two words.

_____

_____

_____

_____

_____   [4]

Total Marks = _____ / 18

Analysing Language 2

Grade 1–3

1 Read the following sentence and give an example of each of the language techniques used in the table below.

The great grinning giant's feet squelched in the mud as he looked danger in the face.

a) alliteration	
b) personification	
c) onomatopoeia	

[3]

Grade 2–4

2 State whether each of the following sentences contains a metaphor or a simile and describe the effect of the comparison.

	Metaphor or simile?	Effect
She came into the room like a tornado.		
You are my rock.		

[4]

Grade 7+

3 Read the following passage from *Wuthering Heights* by Emily Brontë. Here, the narrator visits his landlord's house, Wuthering Heights.

> On that bleak hill-top the earth was hard with a black frost, and the air made me shiver through every limb. Being unable to remove the chain[1], I jumped over, and, running up the flagged causeway[2] bordered with straggling gooseberry bushes, knocked vainly for admittance, till my knuckles tingled, and the dogs howled.
>
> [1] a chain fastening the gate   [2] the path

How does the writer use language to convey an unwelcoming atmosphere?

On a separate piece of paper comment on:

- the writer's choice of words and phrases
- language features and techniques
- sentence forms.

[8]

Total Marks = _____ / 15

Key Technical Skills: Reading

> ## Analysing Form and Structure

Grade 3–5

1 Match the endings **a)**–**c)** with the descriptions **x)**–**z)**.

a) And without hesitation he laid the ancient timepiece in the hands of its rightful owner.

b) Go to your wide futures, you said.

c) Do not play tricks on people unless you can stand the same treatment yourself.

x) Readers might find this ending inspiring.

y) This ending draws a lesson from the story.

z) This is a neat ending that would satisfy the reader.

_____ [3]

Grade 4–6

2 Here is the opening of a short story, 'To Please His Wife', by Thomas Hardy. Read it and answer the questions below.

> The interior of St. James's Church, in Havenpool Town, was slowly darkening under the close clouds of a winter afternoon. It was Sunday: service had just ended, the face of the parson in the pulpit was buried in his hands, and the congregation, with a cheerful sigh of release, were rising from their knees to depart.
>
> For the moment the stillness was so complete that the surging of the sea could be heard outside the harbour-bar. Then it was broken by the footsteps of the clerk going towards the west door to open it in the usual manner for the exit of the assembly. Before, however, he had reached the doorway, the latch was lifted from without, and the dark figure of a man in a sailor's garb appeared against the light.

a) What has just taken place?

_____

b) What do we learn about the story's setting?

_____

c) What is the effect of the phrase, 'slowly darkening under the close clouds of a winter afternoon'?

_____

d) What is the effect of the phrase, 'the stillness was so complete that the surging of the sea could be heard'?

_____

e) Why do you think none of the three people mentioned are given names?

_____

f) What do you think might happen next?

_____ [12]

Total Marks = _____ / 15

GCSE English Workbook

English Language 1

Creative Reading 1

1 Read the extracts below and state which is narrated by...

A A naïve or unreliable narrator

B An omniscient narrator

C A reliable first-person narrator

D An intrusive narrator

a)

> Adam, you perceive, was by no means a marvellous man, nor, properly speaking, a genius, yet I will not pretend that his was an ordinary character among workmen...
>
> From *Adam Bede* by George Eliot

b)

> Feeling the importance of not interrupting Sergeant Cuff's examination of the boy, I received the clerk in another room. He came with bad news of his employer. The agitation and excitement of the last two days had proved too much for Mr Bruff.
>
> From *The Moonstone* by Wilkie Collins

c)

> The Mole was bewitched, entranced, fascinated. By the side of the river he trotted as one trots, when very small, by the side of a man, who holds one spellbound by exciting stories; and when tired at last, he sat on the bank...
>
> From *The Wind in the Willows* by Kenneth Grahame

d)

> After supper she got out her book and learned me about Moses and the Bullrushers; and I was in a sweat to find out all about him; but by and by she let it out that Moses had been dead a considerable long time; so then I didn't care no more about him; because I don't taken no stock in dead people.
>
> From *The Adventures of Huckleberry Finn* by Mark Twain

[4]

Total Marks = _____ / 4

English Language 1

1   Look at the quotations in the table below. Each is taken from one of the set texts, but you do not need to have studied the text to answer the question.

In the third column, enter how we learn about the character, choosing from:

- Narrator's description

- What the character does

- What the character says

- How others react to the character

- What others say to/about the character.

In the fourth column, state what we learn about the character from the quotation.

Character	Quotation	How we learn about the character	What we learn about the character
Lady Catherine de Burgh *Pride and Prejudice*	Her air was not conciliating, nor was her manner of receiving them such as to make her visitors forget their inferior rank.		
Mary Morstan *The Sign of Four*	…I found myself in dream-land, with the sweet face of Mary Morstan looking down upon me.		
Mrs Fairfax *Jane Eyre*	She conducted me to her own chair, and then began to remove my shawl and untie my bonnet strings: I begged she would not give herself so much trouble.		
Fezziwig *A Christmas Carol*	'Yo ho, my boys!' said Fezziwig. 'No more work tonight. Christmas-eve, Dick. Christmas, Ebenezer! Let's have the shutters up…'		
Hyde *The Strange Case of Dr Jekyll and Mr Hyde*	'There must be something else,' said the perplexed gentleman. 'There is something more if I could find a name for it. God bless me, the man hardly seems human!'		

[15]

Total Marks = _____ / 15

English Language 1

Narrative Writing

Imagine you have been set the following task in your exam:

Your school or college is holding a creative writing competition and has invited people to write a short story with the title 'The New Neighbour'.

Use the following questions and guidelines to help you plan your story.

1 **a)** What person will you write the story in: first or third?_____ [1]

   b) If you are writing in the first person, is the narrator also the protagonist?_____ [1]

   c) Who is your protagonist? Make notes about the protagonist:

   i) gender_____

   ii) age_____

   iii) appearance _____

   _____

   iv) background _____

   _____

   v) relationships _____

   _____ [5]

   d) Where is the story set? _____ [1]

   e) When is it set? (Now, in the past or in the future?) _____ [1]

   f) How long does the story take? (A day, a month, a year?) _____ [1]

2 How will your story be structured? Make brief notes on your:

   a) exposition _____

   _____

   b) inciting incident _____

   c) turning point(s) _____

   d) climax _____

   e) coda _____ [10]

Total Marks = _____ / 20

English Language 1

Descriptive Writing

Grade 4–6

Imagine you have been set the following task in your exam:

Your school or college is holding a creative writing competition and has invited people to write a piece of descriptive writing about a place that holds happy memories for them.

Use the following questions and guidelines to help you plan your story.

1   **a)** What person will you write the story in: first or third? _____ [1]

    b) Are you going to write in the past or present tense? _____ [1]

    c) Make brief notes on the place as seen from:

       i) long distance

       _____

       _____

       ii) middle distance

       _____

       _____

       iii) close up

       _____

       _____ [6]

2 Using an adjective and a noun for each, jot down at least two things you can:

    a) see _____

    b) hear _____

    c) smell _____

    d) taste _____

    e) touch _____ [10]

3 Write down an appropriate:

    a) simile _____

    b) metaphor _____ [2]

Total Marks = _____ / 20

English Language 2

Grade 1–6

Reading Non-fiction

1 Read the following two reviews and use the table below to list differences in the writers' points of view and how they are expressed.

A

As soon as I saw Holcombe Manor I felt at home. Of course, it was nothing like our home – rather, it is a quaint half-timbered Tudor house nestling among the gentle hills, surrounded by ancient oaks. There is even a moat. Entering the magnificent hall, heated by a huge welcoming fire, we felt like royalty, and our hosts, Audrey and Frank, treated us like royalty. They gave us a cosy bedroom overlooking the moat, which featured a splendid four-poster bed and led into a delightfully old-fashioned ensuite. Breakfast the next morning was superb, everything sourced from local producers and served in his own inimitable and rather eccentric manner by Frank. Miles from the nearest village, the place exuded tranquillity. It's the perfect place to recharge your batteries.

B

Unless you're some kind of time-traveller and want to experience life in the uncivilised past, avoid Holcombe Manor! For a start, it's miles from the nearest village, which itself doesn't even have a pub or shop. The phone signal is terrible and the ever-so-posh owners haven't even heard of WiFi. Our room was cramped, dominated by a massive ancient, creaky bed, and wasn't as clean as it might be. The bathroom didn't even have a shower. After a poor night's sleep we were treated to a barely adequate breakfast, served up by the bumbling and inefficient 'Lord of the Manor', Frank. We won't be going back.

	Text A	Text B
What is the text about?		
What is the writer's attitude to Holcombe Manor?		
What impression do you get of the writer?		
How would you describe the general tone and style?		
Comment on any interesting language features.		

[20]

Total Marks = _____ / 20

English Language 2

> **Writing Non-fiction**

Grade 3–4 **1** Imagine that in your exam you have been asked to argue for or against the following statement:

'Working hard at school is pointless when you can achieve fame and fortune simply by appearing on reality television.'

In the table, list four or five points that support the statement and four or five points that disagree with the statement.

For	Against

[10]

Grade 4–6 **2** Imagine that the question asked you to write a letter on the subject to a broadsheet newspaper. Write the beginning (salutation) and first paragraph of your letter.

_____

_____

_____

_____

_____

_____

[5]

Grade 4–6 **3** Imagine that the question asked you to write an article for a teenage magazine. Write the first part of your answer.

_____

_____

_____

_____

_____

[5]

Total Marks = ... / 20

Shakespeare

Context and Themes

1 Think about the Shakespeare play you have studied (*Macbeth, Romeo and Juliet, The Merchant of Venice, Much Ado About Nothing, The Tempest* or *Julius Caesar*). Write a sentence or two explaining how each of the following themes is reflected in it. An example has been done for you.

a) Power and ambition – **Example:** Macbeth and Lady Macbeth ruthlessly achieve their ambition to make Macbeth king but Macbeth is corrupted by his power.

b) Love and marriage _____

_____

c) Order and chaos _____

_____

d) Fate _____

_____

e) Revenge _____

_____

f) Appearance and reality _____

_____ [10]

2 Think about the play you have studied and write a sentence or two explaining how each of the following aspects of social and historical context is reflected in it. An example has been done for you.

a) The place where the play is set – **Example:** Venice was a great port and commercial centre, its success founded on the risks taken by merchants, as in *The Merchant of Venice*.

b) Religion _____

_____

c) Male and female roles _____

_____

d) Cultural context _____

_____

e) Wealth and poverty/social class _____

_____

f) Real historical events _____

_____ [10]

Total Marks = _____ / 20

Shakespeare

Characters, Language and Structure

 Grade 3–6

1 Choose two characters from the play you have studied. Find a quotation (either words spoken by the character or words spoken about the character) which tells us something about each character.

Put the characters' names, quotations and a brief explanation of what you think the quotations tell us about the character in the table below. An example has been done for you.

Character	Quotation	Explanation
Cassius	CAESAR: Yon Cassius has a lean and hungry look. He thinks too much. Such men are dangerous. (*Julius Caesar* Act 1 Scene 2)	Having said that he prefers men who are 'fat' because they are content, Caesar says that 'lean' Cassius, who is 'hungry' or ambitious, cannot be trusted.

[8]

Grade 3–6

2 Here are some quotations from Shakespeare that use the following literary techniques: **metaphor, oxymoron, simile, rhetorical question**.

For each quotation, state which technique is being used and its effect.

a) Shall I lay perjury upon my soul?

No, not for Venice. (*The Merchant of Venice* Act 4 Scene 1)

Technique: _____ Effect: _____

_____

b) O heavy lightness, serious vanity (*Romeo and Juliet*, Act 1 Scene 1)

Technique: _____ Effect: _____

_____

c) The strongest oaths are straw

To the fire i' the blood (*The Tempest* Act 4 Scene 1)

Technique: _____ Effect: _____

_____

d) DUNCAN: Dismayed not this our captains, Macbeth and Banquo?

CAPTAIN: Yes, as sparrows eagles, or the hare the lion! (*Macbeth* Act 1 Scene 2)

Technique: _____ Effect: _____ [12]

_____

Total Marks = _____ / 20

The 19th-Century Novel

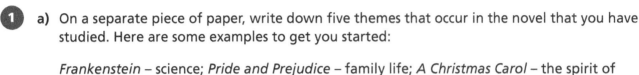

Context and Themes

Grade 4–6

1 **a)** On a separate piece of paper, write down five themes that occur in the novel that you have studied. Here are some examples to get you started:

Frankenstein – science; *Pride and Prejudice* – family life; *A Christmas Carol* – the spirit of Christmas; *Jane Eyre* – marriage; *Great Expectations* – money; *The Strange Case of Dr Jekyll and Mr Hyde* – good and evil; *The Sign of Four* – treasure. [5]

b) Now write a sentence or two about each theme that you have identified, for example:

Frankenstein explores the possible consequences of scientific discovery, as Frankenstein unwittingly creates an evil 'creature'. [10]

Grade 5–6

2 Read the following statements about nineteenth-century society and write a sentence or two explaining how each one is reflected in the novel you have studied.

a) Almost everyone was Christian so writers could assume that readers shared Christian beliefs and values.

Example: Jane Eyre is horrified at the idea of marrying a man who is already married. The fact that she discovers Rochester is married in church emphasises the sinful nature of what he is doing.

_____

_____

b) Nineteenth-century writers were interested in both personal feelings and moral responsibility.

_____

_____

c) Nineteenth-century women had fewer rights than men and fewer opportunities.

_____

_____

d) The nineteenth century was a time of exploration, discovery and scientific advances.

_____

_____

e) While a few people were very rich in nineteenth-century Britain, many lived in poverty.

_____

_____ [10]

Total Marks = _____ / 25

Characters, Language and Structure

Grade 4–6

1 Identify five significant characters from the novel you have studied. For each one, draw up a chart like the one below and fill it in.

Name	
Description/ Appearance	
Background	
Personality	
Relationships	
Function	

[25]

Grade 4–6

2 Here are five quotations from nineteenth-century novels. Each uses a linguistic/literary technique. Match each quotation **a)–e)** with a description of its use **v)–z)**.

a) [I] managed to compound a drug by which these powers should be dethroned from their supremacy. (*The Strange Case of Dr Jekyll and Mr Hyde*)

b) 'Bah!' said Scrooge, 'Humbug!' (*A Christmas Carol*, Stave 1)

c) '... the offered olive-branch.' (*Pride and Prejudice*, Chapter 13)

d) 'Hold her arms, Miss Abbot; she's like a mad cat.' (*Jane Eyre*, Chapter 2)

e) How can I describe my emotions at this catastrophe, or how delineate the wretch whom with such infinite pains and care I had endeavoured to form? (*Frankenstein*, Chapter 5)

v) The character uses a colloquial metaphor to express his strong feelings.

w) The speaker uses a simile to describe the violent resistance of someone being restrained.

x) The narrator uses a rhetorical question before attempting to answer it himself.

y) The narrator combines scientific language and personification to describe his attempt to change his nature.

z) The letter-writer uses a symbol that is commonly recognised as representing an offer of peace.

[5]

Total Marks = _____ / 30

Modern Texts

Context and Themes

1 Think about the text you have studied and its social and cultural context. In answer to each of these questions, circle the most appropriate answer. If you have studied the anthology you may be able to answer these questions for individual stories.

a) When was the text written?   **1940s**   **1950s**   **1980s**   **1990s**   **2000s**   **2010s**

b) When is it set?   **At the time it was written**   **Before the time it was written**
   After the time it was written

c) Where is it set? (more than one answer possible)
Northern England   **The Midlands**   **London/Southern England**   **On a farm**
   In a town/city   **In a village**   **In a school**

d) How would you describe its genre/form? (more than one answer possible)
Musical theatre   **Science fiction**   **Allegory**   **Novel**   **Drama**
   Short story   **Bildungsroman**

e) For what audience was it written?   **Adults**   **Children/teenagers**   [5]

2 a) Write a paragraph about the 'world' of the text you have studied, referring to where and when it is set, how the characters live and how their attitudes reflect the time and place in which they live.

_____

_____

_____

_____ [5]

b) Write a paragraph explaining how the world of the text differs from the world in which you live.

_____

_____

_____

_____ [5]

3 In the table below, write three themes that occur in your text and a sentence or two about each theme.

Theme	Explanation

[9]

Total Marks = _____ / 24

Modern Texts

Characters, Language and Structure

Grade 3–5

1 If you have studied a novel or short stories, answer only questions **a)–e)** about language and structure. (If you have studied the stories in the anthology, answer separately on each story you have studied.) If you have studied a play, answer only questions **f)–j)**.

a) How is your text divided? _____

b) How would you describe the narrator? _____

c) How would you describe the language/register used by the narrator? _____
_____

d) Have you noticed anything interesting about how any of the characters speak?
_____

e) Find an example of the use of figurative language in your text. _____
_____ **[5]**

f) How is the play divided? _____

g) What do we learn from the stage directions? _____
_____

h) Which characters, if any, speak directly to the audience? _____
_____

i) Are there any notable differences between the ways in which different characters speak?
_____

j) Find an example of the use of figurative language in your text. _____
_____ **[5]**

Grade 4–6

2 Identify five significant characters from the text you have studied. For each one, draw up a chart like the one below and fill it in.

Name	
Description/Appearance	
Background	
Personality	
Relationships	
Function	

[25]

Total Marks = _____ / 30

Poetry

Context and Themes

If you have studied the 'Love and Relationships' cluster in the anthology, answer only questions **1** and **3**.
If you have studied 'Power and Conflict' answer only questions **2** and **4**.

Grade 2–4

1 Match poems **a)–e)** with the descriptions of aspects of their context **v)–z)**.

a) 'Follower'	**v)** Nineteenth-century interest in psychology.
b) 'Before You Were Mine'	**w)** Twentieth-century rural Ireland.
c) 'Porphyria's Lover'	**x)** Twentieth-century Scotland.
d) 'Singh Song!'	**y)** Women's experience in rural England.
e) 'The Farmer's Bride'	**z)** The Sikh community in England.

[5]

Grade 2–4

2 Match poems **a)–e)** with the descriptions of aspects of their context **v)–z)**.

a) 'London'	**v)** The history of the Caribbean.
b) 'The Charge of the Light Brigade'	**w)** Poverty and revolution.
c) 'Checking Out Me History'	**x)** The Romantic movement.
d) 'Poppies'	**y)** Remembrance Sunday.
e) Extract from 'The Prelude'	**z)** The Crimean War.

[5]

Grade 2–3

3 In which poems in 'Love and Relationships' are these themes present? Try to name three.

a) Marriage _____

b) Parents and children _____

c) Romantic love _____

d) Nature _____

e) Death _____ [15]

Grade 2–3

4 In which poems in 'Power and Conflict' are these themes present? Try to name three.

a) Soldiers at war _____

b) The effect of war on non-combatants _____

c) The abuse of power _____

d) Memories _____

e) Nature _____ [15]

Total Marks = _____ / 20

Poetry

Language, Form and Structure

If you have studied the 'Love and Relationships' cluster in the anthology, answer only questions **1** and **3**. If you have studied 'Power and Conflict', answer questions **2** and **4**.

Grade 2–3

1 Which poems in 'Love and Relationships' feature the following aspects of form and structure?

   a) Sonnet form _____

   b) Ballad form _____

   c) Rhyming couplets _____

   d) Half rhyme _____ **[4]**

Grade 2–3

2 Which poems in 'Power and Conflict' feature the following aspects of form and structure?

   a) Iambic pentameter _____

   b) Ballad form _____

   c) Rhyming couplets _____

   d) Refrain _____ **[4]**

Grade 4–6

3 Look at these quotations from poems in 'Love and Relationships'. On a separate piece of paper, identify the literary techniques they use and explain their effect. Pick from these techniques: **alliteration; archaic language; metaphor; onomatopoeia; pathetic fallacy; repetition; sibilance.**

Some quotations may include more than one technique.

   a) And a few leaves lay on the starving sod ('Neutral Tones')

   b) ...Anchor. Kite. ('Mother, any distance')

   c) Long, long shall I rue thee ('When We Two Parted')

   d) ...your ghost clatters towards me... ('Before You Were Mine') **[16]**

Grade 4–6

4 Look at these quotations from poems in 'Power and Conflict'. On a separate piece of paper, identify the literary techniques they use and explain their effect. Pick from these techniques: **assonance; dialect; pathetic fallacy; repetition; simile.**

Some quotations may include more than one technique.

   a) His foot hung like/Statuary in mid-stride. ('Bayonet Charge')

   b) And, as I rose upon the stroke, my boat
      Went heaving through the water like a swan. (Extract from 'The Prelude')

   c) Dem tell me/Dem tell me/Wha dem want to tell me. ('Checking Out Me History')

   d) leaves and branches/can raise a tragic chorus in a gale. ('Storm on the Island') **[16]**

Total Marks = _____ / 20

Poetry

Unseen Poetry

1 Read the poem below and answer the questions that follow. Continue on a separate piece of paper if needed.

> **A Birthday** by Christina Rossetti
>
> My heart is like a singing bird
>   Whose nest is in a watered shoot;
> My heart is like an apple-tree
>   Whose boughs are bent with thick-set fruit;
> My heart is like a rainbow shell
>   That paddles in a halcyon sea;
> My heart is gladder than all these
>   Because my love is come to me.
>
> Raise me a dais of silk and down;
>   Hang it with vair[1] and purple dyes;
> Carve it in doves and pomegranates,
>   And peacocks with a hundred eyes;
> Work it in gold and silver grapes,
>   In leaves and silver fleurs-de-lys;
> Because the birthday of my life
>   Is come, my love is come to me.
>
> [1] a bluish grey fur

a) What is the poem about according to the title? _____

b) What is it actually about? _____

c) Is there a regular rhythm and/or rhyme scheme? If so, what effect does it have?

_____

d) What does the poet mean by her 'heart'? _____

e) What is the effect of the repetition of 'my heart' in the first stanza? _____

_____

f) Which three things does she use similes to compare her 'heart' to and what links them?

_____

g) What general impression do the images of the second stanza give? _____

_____

h) Identify three imperatives in the second stanza and describe their effect. _____

_____

i) How would you describe the poet's mood? _____

j) What is meant by the final two lines? _____

_____ [10]

Poetry

2   Read this poem. Then re-read the poem on page 175 and compare the poems using the table below.

> **On His Eightieth Birthday** by Robert Savage Landor
>
> To my ninth decade I have tottered on,
> And no soft arm bends now my steps to steady;
> She, who once led me where she would, is gone,
> So when he calls me, Death shall find me ready.

	'A Birthday'	'On His Eightieth Birthday'
Speaker or voice		
Structure		
Rhythm/metre		
Rhyme		
Vocabulary/register		
Use of sound		
Imagery		
Themes		
The poet's attitude		

[36]

Total Marks = _____ / 46

English Language Paper 1

Explorations in Creative Reading and Writing

You are advised to spend about 15 minutes reading through the source and all five questions.
You should make sure you leave sufficient time to check your answers.

Section A: Reading

Answer all questions in this section.
You are advised to spend about 45 minutes on this section.

Source

This extract is taken from 'The Postmaster', a short story by Rabindranath Tagore, first published in 1891. The story, about a man who runs the post office, is set in a village in India.

> Our postmaster belonged to Calcutta[1]. He felt like a fish out of water in this remote village. His office and living-room were in a dark thatched shed, not far from a green, slimy pond, surrounded on all sides by a dense growth.
>
> The postmaster's salary was small. He had to cook his own meals, which he used to share with
> 5 Ratan, an orphan girl of the village, who did odd jobs for him.
>
> When in the evening the smoke began to curl up from the village cowsheds, and the cicadas[4] chirped in every bush; when the mendicants of the Baül sect[3] sang their shrill songs in their daily meeting-place, when any poet, who had attempted to watch the movement of the leaves in the dense bamboo thickets, would have felt a ghostly shiver run down his back, the postmaster would
> 10 light his little lamp, and call out "Ratan."
>
> Ratan would sit outside waiting for this call, and, instead of coming in at once, would reply, "Did you call me, sir?"
>
> "What are you doing?" the postmaster would ask.
>
> "I must be going to light the kitchen fire," would be the answer.
>
> 15 And the postmaster would say: "Oh, let the kitchen fire be for awhile; light me my pipe first."
>
> At last Ratan would enter, with puffed-out cheeks, vigorously blowing into a flame a live coal to light the tobacco. This would give the postmaster an opportunity of conversing. "Well, Ratan," perhaps he would begin, "do you remember anything of your mother?" That was a fertile subject. Ratan partly remembered, and partly didn't. Her father had been fonder of her than her mother;
> 20 him she recollected more vividly. He used to come home in the evening after his work, and one or two evenings stood out more clearly than others, like pictures in her memory. Ratan would sit on the floor near the postmaster's feet, as memories crowded in upon her. She called to mind a little brother that she had—and how on some bygone cloudy day she had played at fishing with him on the edge of the pond, with a twig for a make-believe fishing-rod. Such little incidents
> 25 would drive out greater events from her mind. Thus, as they talked, it would often get very late, and the postmaster would feel too lazy to do any cooking at all. Ratan would then hastily light the fire, and toast some unleavened bread, which, with the cold remnants of the morning meal, was enough for their supper.

On some evenings, seated at his desk in the corner of the big empty shed, the postmaster too
30 would call up memories of his own home, of his mother and his sister, of those for whom in his
exile his heart was sad,—memories which were always haunting him, but which he could not talk
about with the men of the factory, though he found himself naturally recalling them aloud in the
presence of the simple little girl. And so it came about that the girl would allude to his people
as mother, brother, and sister, as if she had known them all her life. In fact, she had a complete
35 picture of each one of them painted in her little heart.

One noon, during a break in the rains, there was a cool soft breeze blowing; the smell of the
damp grass and leaves in the hot sun felt like the warm breathing of the tired earth on one's body.
A persistent bird went on all the afternoon repeating the burden of its one complaint in Nature's
audience chamber.

40 The postmaster had nothing to do. The shimmer of the freshly washed leaves, and the banked-
up remnants of the retreating rain-clouds were sights to see; and the postmaster was watching
them and thinking to himself: "Oh, if only some kindred soul were near—just one loving human
being whom I could hold near my heart!" This was exactly, he went on to think, what that bird
was trying to say, and it was the same feeling which the murmuring leaves were striving to express.
45 But no one knows, or would believe, that such an idea might also take possession of an ill-paid
village postmaster in the deep, silent mid-day interval of his work.

The postmaster sighed, and called out "Ratan." Ratan was then sprawling beneath the guava-
tree, busily engaged in eating unripe guavas. At the voice of her master, she ran up breathlessly,
saying: "Were you calling me, Dada?" "I was thinking," said the postmaster, "of teaching you to
50 read." And then for the rest of the afternoon he taught her the alphabet.

[1] now called Kolkata

[2] insects, which make a loud buzzing noise

[3] a group of religious wandering musicians

---

1 Read again the beginning of the source from line 1 to 5.

List four things you learn about the postmaster from this part of the source.   **[4 marks]**

---

2 Look in detail at this extract from line 6 to 10 of the source.

> When in the evening the smoke began to curl up from the village cowsheds, and the cicadas[4]
> chirped in every bush; when the mendicants[3] of the Baül sect sang their shrill songs in their daily
> meeting-place, when any poet, who had attempted to watch the movement of the leaves in the
> dense bamboo thickets, would have felt a ghostly shiver run down his back, the postmaster would
> light his little lamp, and call out "Ratan."

How does the writer use language here to create an impression of evening in the village?

You could include the writer's choice of:

- words and phrases
- language features and techniques
- sentence forms.   **[8 marks]**

3 You now need to think about the whole source.

This text is from the beginning of a short story.

How has the writer structured the text to interest you as a reader?

You could write about:

- what the writer focuses your attention on at the beginning of the source
- how and why the writer changes this focus as the source develops
- any other structural features that interest you.   **[8 marks]**

4 A student said, 'The writer has created a touching story about two lonely people helping each other. Ratan appears to get more out of the relationship than the postmaster.'

To what extent do you agree?

In your response you could:

- consider your own impressions of the postmaster, Ratan and their relationship
- evaluate how the writer conveys ideas about, and attitudes to, loneliness
- support your response with references to the text.   **[20 marks]**

Section B: Writing

You are advised to spend about 45 minutes on this section.
You are reminded of the need to plan your answers.
Write in full sentences.
You should leave enough time to check your work at the end.

5 A local newspaper is running a creative writing competition and intends to publish the winning entries.

EITHER

(a) Write a description of a place suggested by this picture.

OR

(b) Write a story that begins 'Suddenly the quiet of the evening was interrupted by an unfamiliar sound.'

[24 marks for content and organisation and 16 marks for technical accuracy: total 40 marks]

English Language Paper 2

Writers' Viewpoints and Perspectives

You are advised to spend about 15 minutes reading through the source and all five questions.
You should make sure you leave sufficient time to check your answers.

Section A: Reading

Answer all questions in this section.
You are advised to spend about 45 minutes on this section.

Source A

This extract is taken from *Domestic Manners of the Americans* by Frances Trollope, published in 1832. In this chapter the writer, an Englishwoman living in the USA, gives her reaction to what she sees as the 'familiarity' of Americans.

The extraordinary familiarity of our poor neighbours startled us at first, and we hardly knew how to receive their uncouth advances, or what was expected of us in return; however, it sometimes produced very laughable scenes. Upon one occasion two of my children set off upon an exploring walk up the hills; they were absent rather longer than we expected, and the rest of
5 our party determined upon going out to meet them; we knew the direction they had taken, but thought it would be as well to enquire at a little public-house at the bottom of the hill, if such a pair had been seen to pass. A woman, whose appearance more resembled a Covent Garden market-woman than any thing else I can remember, came out and answered my question with the most jovial good humour in the affirmative, and prepared to join us in our search. Her look,
10 her voice, her manner, were so exceedingly coarse and vehement, that she almost frightened me; she passed her arm within mine, and to the inexpressible amusement of my young people, she dragged me on, talking and questioning me without ceasing. She lived but a short distance from us, and I am sure intended to be a very good neighbour; but her violent intimacy made me dread to pass her door; my children, including my sons, she always addressed by their Christian
15 names, excepting when she substituted the word "honey;" this familiarity of address, however, I afterwards found was universal throughout all ranks in the United States.

My general appellation amongst my neighbours was "the English old woman," but in mentioning each other they constantly employed the term "lady;" and they evidently had a pleasure in using it, for I repeatedly observed, that in speaking of a neighbour, instead of saying
20 Mrs. Such-a-one, they described her as "the lady over the way what takes in washing," or as "that there lady, out by the Gulley, what is making dip-candles." Mr. Trollope was as constantly called "the old man," while draymen, butchers' boys, and the labourers on the canal were invariably denominated "them gentlemen;" nay, we once saw one of the most gentlemanlike men in Cincinnati introduce a fellow in dirty shirt sleeves, and all sorts of detestable et cetera, to one of
25 his friends, with this formula, "D— let me introduce this gentleman to you." Our respective titles certainly were not very important; but the eternal shaking hands with these ladies and gentlemen was really an annoyance, and the more so, as the near approach of the gentlemen was always redolent of whiskey and tobacco.

Source B

A newspaper article in which the writer expresses his opinion about customer service in restaurants.

CALL ME (SIR OR) MADAM

Sean Boyle wants to be served by a waiter, not a new best friend.

'Hey, guys! How are you doing?'

The first time I was greeted like this by a waiter in a (fairly upmarket) restaurant, I was outraged.
5   Obviously not a very classy joint, I thought, and not one I would care to set foot in again. But it's got to the point now that if I stuck to my guns and boycotted every establishment where I was spoken to like a New York delinquent rather than a middle-aged British gentleman, I would never leave the house.

And what is it about the word 'guys'? Suddenly, it's everywhere, applied to people of both genders and all ages. It started with children's T.V. presenters, ever notorious for using Americanisms to 'get down
10 with the kids', and now it's everywhere. On television it's used to address not just hip young men from the streets but elderly ladies buying antiques, minor celebrities learning to dance and even elected politicians. Go into any school nowadays and you're likely to hear the appalling Americanism, 'Listen up, guys' rather than, 'Pay attention, children' or 'Be quiet, Class Four'. Whenever more than one person is addressed they are called 'you guys'. It's as if nobody is aware that the plural form of the pronoun 'you' is 'you'.

15 This kind of over-familiarity seems to have been imported from America – or copied from American films and television. Yet – to bring us back to restaurants – friends who have lived in the USA tell me that Americans are often more polite and formal than we are: being addressed as 'Sir' or 'Madam' is the norm. Of course, you can get the forced friendliness of 'Hi, my name's Heidi. I'll be your server tonight.' That's another irritating trend that's gaining a foothold over here – we don't need to know her name
20 and we already know what her job is. We're not here to get chummy with the staff; we just want them to bring us our food. And when it happens in a British restaurant it just seems false. What we've imported is a stereotypical idea of Stateside friendliness rather than genuine warmth and good manners.

I wonder if this need to embrace informality has something to do with a British dislike of servility. I used to work in a shop in London and – like most of my colleagues – was quite happy to
25 address customers as 'Sir' or 'Madam'. Yet I knew people who said they found this demeaning, as if by addressing people in this way we were accepting that they were somehow superior to us.

It has been said this discomfort with the idea of serving others is a reaction to the time when huge numbers of working-class Britons spent their lives 'in service', often in 'Downton Abbey' style big houses, where they were never allowed to forget their lowly status. Twenty-first-century Britons bow to
30 no-one. In contrast, in countries like France and Italy, serving people is not considered demeaning. To serve is not to be servile. Walk into almost any restaurant in these countries and you will be greeted by 'bonjour' or 'buona sera' and addressed as 'Monsieur/Madame' or 'Signore/Signora'. In return, you are expected to greet not only the staff but the people sitting near you. When you've done that, you can get on with eating your meal, efficiently served by a professional waiter – not by your new best friend, Luigi.

35 I don't want waiting staff and bar staff to touch their forelocks and grovel to me. But nor do I want my evening out to turn into some kind of pseudo-American sitcom. There's a happy medium here, 'guys'. By all means be friendly – there's nothing wrong with a cheerful smile as you say 'good evening' or even a brief chat about the weather – but treat your customers with respect, starting with the use of 'Sir' and 'Madam'. And for the sake of good customer relations, the English
40 language and my blood pressure, please never, ever call us 'you guys'.

1. Read again the first paragraph of **Source A** (lines 1 to 16).

Choose **four** statements below which are TRUE.

- Shade the boxes of the ones that you think are true.
- Choose a maximum of four statements.

A. The neighbours are very unfriendly.

B. Frances Trollope has more than two children.

C. She knows which way the children went.

D. The woman says she has not seen the children.

E. The woman is quiet and gentle.

F. Trollope's children find the incident funny.

G. The neighbour calls Trollope's children by their first names.

H. The woman's familiarity is unusual in America.

[4 marks]

2. You need to refer to **Source A** and **Source B** for this question.

Use details from both sources. Write a summary of the differences and similarities between the behaviour described by Trollope and by Boyle. **[8 marks]**

3. You now need to refer **only** to **Source A**, the extract from *Domestic Manners of the Americans*.

How does the writer use language to inform and entertain the reader? **[12 marks]**

4. For this question, you need to refer to both **Source A** and **Source B**.

Compare how the writers convey their attitudes to good manners and over-friendliness. In your answer you should:

- compare their attitudes
- compare the methods they use to convey these attitudes
- support your ideas with quotations from both texts. **[16 marks]**

Section B: Writing

You are advised to spend about 45 minutes on this section.
You are reminded of the need to plan your answers.
Write in full sentences.
You should leave enough time to check your work at the end.

5. 'People claim that they have hundreds or even thousands of friends – but they've never met most of them. In real life, nobody has more than two or three true friends.'

Write an article for a magazine in which you explain your point of view on this statement.

[24 marks for content and organisation and 16 marks for technical accuracy: total 40 marks]

English Literature Paper 1

Shakespeare and the 19th-Century Novel

You should spend a total of 1 hour 45 minutes on this paper.
Answer **one** question from **Section A** and **one** question from **Section B**.
The maximum mark for the paper is 64.
Spelling, punctuation and grammar (AO4) will be assessed in **Section A**. There are four additional marks available.

Section A: Shakespeare

Choose the question from this section on your chosen text.

1 *Macbeth*

Read the following extract from Act 4 Scene 3 and then answer the question that follows.

At this point in the play, Malcolm has just told Macduff that his family has been killed on Macbeth's orders.

	MACDUFF	He has no children. All my pretty ones!
		Did you say all? O hell-kite! All?
		What, all my pretty chickens and their dam
		At one fell swoop?
5	**MALCOLM**	Dispute it like a man.
	MACDUFF	I shall do so,
		But I must also feel it as a man.
		I cannot but remember such things were
		That were most precious to me. Did heaven look on
10		And would not take their part? Sinful Macduff,
		They were all struck for thee. Naught that I am,
		Not for their own demerits but for mine
		Fell slaughter on their souls. Heaven rest them now.
	MALCOLM	Be this the whetstone of your sword. Let grief
15		Convert to anger: blunt not the heart, enrage it.
	MACDUFF	O, I could play the woman with mine eyes
		And braggart with my tongue! But gentle heavens
		Cut short all intermission. Front to front
		Bring thou this fiend of Scotland and myself.
20		Within my sword's length set him. If he 'scape,
		Heaven forgive him too.

Starting with this extract, explore how Shakespeare presents Macduff's character in *Macbeth*.

Write about:

• how Shakespeare presents Macduff in this extract
• how Shakespeare presents Macduff in the play as a whole.

[30 marks + AO4 4 marks]

2 *Romeo and Juliet*

Read the following extract from Act 2 Scene 3 and then answer the question that follows.

Here, Friar Laurence reacts to the news that Romeo has fallen in love with Juliet.

	FRIAR LAURENCE	Holy Saint Francis, what a change is here!
		Is Rosaline that thou didst love so dear,
		So soon forsaken? Young men's love then lies
		Not truly in their hearts but in their eyes.
5		Jesu Maria, what a deal of brine
		Hath washed thy sallow cheek for Rosaline!
		How much salt water thrown away in waste
		To season love, that of it doth not taste!
		The sun not yet thy sighs from heaven clears.
10		Thy old groans yet ring in my ancient ears.
		Lo, here upon thy cheek the stain doth sit
		Of an old tear that is not washed off yet.
		If e'er thou wast thyself, and those woes thine,
		Thou and these woes were all for Rosaline.
15		And art thou changed? Pronounce this sentence then:
		Women may fall when there's no strength in men.
	ROMEO	Thou chidd'st me oft for loving Rosaline.
	FRIAR LAURENCE	For doting, not for loving, pupil mine.

Starting with this extract, explore how Shakespeare presents attitudes to love in *Romeo and Juliet*.

Write about:

- how Shakespeare presents attitudes to love in this extract
- how Shakespeare presents attitudes to love in the play as a whole.

[30 marks + AO4 4 marks]

3 *The Tempest*

Read the following extract from Act 2 Scene 2 and then answer the question that follows.

In this scene, Stefano and Trinculo have made Caliban drunk and he has sworn to serve Stefano instead of Prospero.

	CALIBAN	I prithee, let me bring thee where crabs grow,
		And I with my long nails will dig thee pig-nuts.
		Show thee a jay's nest, and instruct thee how
		To snare the nimble marmoset. I'll bring thee
5		To clust'ring filberts, and sometimes I'll get thee
		Young seamews from the rock. Wilt thou go with me?

STEFANO	I prithee now, lead the way, without any more talking. Trinculo, the King and all our company else being drowned, we will inherit here. Here, bear my bottle. Fellow Trinculo, we'll fill him by and by again.
10 **CALIBAN** (*sings drunkenly*)	Farewell, master, farewell, farewell!
TRINCULO	A howling monster, a drunken monster!
CALIBAN (*sings*)	No more dams I'll make for fish.
	Nor fetch in firing.
	At requiring,
15	Nor scrape trenchering, nor wash dish.
	'Ban, 'ban, Cacaliban.
	Has a new master. Get a new man!
	Freedom, high-day! High-day, freedom! Freedom, high-day, freedom!

Starting with this extract, explore how Shakespeare writes about slavery and freedom in *The Tempest*.

Write about:

- how Shakespeare presents ideas about slavery and freedom in this extract
- how Shakespeare presents ideas about slavery and freedom in the play as a whole.

[30 marks + AO4 4 marks]

4 | *Much Ado About Nothing*

Read the following extract from Act 1 Scene 3 and then answer the question that follows.

Here, Don John discusses his sad mood and discontent with Conrad.

	DON JOHN	I cannot hide what I am. I must be sad when I have cause, and smile at no man's jests; eat when I have stomach, and wait for no man's leisure; sleep when I am drowsy, and tend on no man's business; laugh when I am merry, and claw no man in his humour.
5	**CONRAD**	Yea, but you must not make the full show of this till you may do it without controlment. You have of late stood out against your brother, and he hath ta'en you newly into his grace, where it is impossible you should take true root but by the fair weather that you make yourself. It is needful that you frame the season for your own harvest.
10	**DON JOHN**	I had rather be a canker in a hedge than a rose in his grace, and it better fits my blood to be disdained of all than to fashion a carriage to rob love from any. In this, though I cannot be said to be a flattering honest man, it must not be denied but I am a plain-dealing villain. I am trusted with a muzzle, and enfranchised with a clog. Therefore I have decreed not to sing in my cage. If I had my mouth I would bite. If I had my liberty I would do my liking. In the meantime, let me be that I am, and seek not to alter me.

Starting with this extract, explore how Shakespeare presents Don John as a villain in *Much Ado About Nothing*.

Write about:

- how Shakespeare presents Don John in this extract
- how Shakespeare presents Don John in the play as a whole.

[30 marks + AO4 4 marks]

5 *The Merchant of Venice*

Read the following extract from Act 3 Scene 2 and then answer the question that follows.

Here, Portia explains her feelings to Bassanio before he chooses a casket.

PORTIA		I pray you tarry. Pause a day or two
		Before you hazard, for in choosing wrong
		I lose your company; therefore forbear a while.
		There's something tells me, but it is not love.
5		I would not lose you; and you know yourself
		Hate counsels not in such a quality.
		But lest you should not understand me well –
		And yet a maiden hath no tongue but thought –
		I would detain you here some month or two
10		Before you venture for me. I could teach you
		How to choose right, but then I am forsworn.
		So will I never be. So may you miss me;
		But if you do, you'll make me wish a sin,
		That I had been forsworn. Beshrew your eyes!
15		They have o'erlooked me and divided me:
		One half of me is yours, the other half yours –
		Mine own, I would say—but if mine, then yours,
		And so all yours. O these naughty times
		Put bars between the owners and their rights!
20		And so though yours, not yours. Prove it so.
		Let Fortune go to hell for it, not I.

Starting with this extract, explore how Shakespeare presents the role of women in *The Merchant of Venice*.

Write about:

- how Shakespeare presents the role of women in this speech
- how Shakespeare presents the role of women in the play as a whole.

[30 marks + AO4 4 marks]

6 *Julius Caesar*

Read the following extract from Act 5 Scene 5 and then answer the question that follows.

At this point in the play, after losing the final battle, Brutus has killed himself.

MESSALA	How died my master, Strato?
STRATO	I held his sword, and he did run upon it.
MESSALA	Octavius, then take him to follow thee,
	That did the latest service to my master.
5 ANTONY	This was the noblest Roman of them all.
	All the conspirators save only he
	Did that they did in envy of great Caesar.
	He only in a general honest thought
	And common good to all made one of them.
10	His life was gentle, and the elements
	So mixed in him that nature might stand up
	And say to all the world 'This was a man'.
OCTAVIUS	According to his virtue let us use him,
	With all respect and rites of burial.
15	Within my tent his bones tonight shall lie,
	Most like a soldier, ordered honourably.

Starting with this extract, explore how Shakespeare presents Brutus as 'the noblest Roman of them all' in *Julius Caesar*.

Write about:

- how Shakespeare presents Brutus in this extract
- how Shakespeare presents Brutus in the play as a whole.

[30 marks + AO4 4 marks]

Section B: The 19th-Century Novel

Choose the question from this section on your chosen text.

7 **Robert Louis Stevenson: *The Strange Case of Dr Jekyll and Mr Hyde***

Read the following extract from Chapter 7 and then answer the question that follows.

In this extract, Mr Utterson and Mr Enfield see Dr Jekyll at his window.

The court was very cool and a little damp. And full of premature twilight, although the sky, high up overhead, was still bright with sunset. The middle one of the three windows was halfway open; and sitting close beside it, taking the air with an infinite sadness of mien, like some disconsolate prisoner, Utterson saw Dr Jekyll.

5 'What! Jekyll!' he cried. 'I trust you are better.'

'I am very low, Utterson,' replied the doctor drearily, 'very low. It will not last long, thank God.'

'You stay too much indoors,' said the lawyer. 'You should be out, whipping up the circulation, like Mr Enfield and me. (This is my cousin – Mr Enfield – Dr Jekyll.) Come now; get your hat and take a quick turn with us.'

10   'You are very good,' sighed the other. 'I should like to very much; but no, no, no, it is quite impossible; I dare not, But indeed, Utterson, I am very glad to see you; this is really a great pleasure; I would ask you and Mr Enfield up, but the place is really not fit.'

'Why then,' said the lawyer, good-naturedly, 'the best thing we can do is to stay down here and speak to you from where we are.'

15   'That is just what I was about to venture to propose,' returned the doctor with a smile. But the words were hardly uttered, before the smile was struck out of his face and succeeded by an expression of such abject terror and despair, as froze the very blood of the two gentlemen below. They saw it but for a glimpse, for the window was instantly thrust down; but that glance had been sufficient, and they turned and left the court without a word.

Starting with this extract, write about how sympathetically Stevenson presents the character of Dr Jekyll in *The Strange Case of Doctor Jekyll and Mr Hyde*.

Write about:

- how Stevenson writes about Jekyll and how others react to him in this extract
- how he writes about Jekyll in the novel as a whole.   **[30 marks]**

8 **Charles Dickens: *A Christmas Carol***

Read the following extract from Stave (Chapter) 4 and then answer the question that follows.

In this extract, Scrooge is watching the Cratchits after the 'death' of Tiny Tim.

She hurried out to meet him; and little Bob in his comforter – he had need of it poor fellow – came in. His tea was ready for him on the hob, and they all tried who should help him to it most. Then the two young Cratchits got upon his knees, and laid, each child, a little cheek against his face, as if they said, 'Don't mind it, father. Don't be grieved!'

5   Bob was very cheerful with them, and spoke pleasantly to all the family. He looked at the work upon the table, and praised the industry and speed of Mrs Cratchit and the girls. They would be done long before Sunday, he said.

'Sunday! You went today, then, Robert?' said his wife.

'Yes, my dear,' returned Bob. 'I wish you could have gone. It would have done you good to see
10 how green a place it is. But you'll see it often. I promised him that I would walk there on a Sunday. My little, little child!' cried Bob. 'My little child!' He broke down all at once. He couldn't help it. If he could have helped it, he and his child would have been farther apart, perhaps, than they were.

He left the room, and went upstairs into the room above, which was lighted cheerfully, and hung with Christmas. There was a chair set close beside the child, and there were signs of
15 someone having been there lately. Poor Bob sat down in it, and, when he had thought a little and composed himself, he kissed the little face. He was reconciled to what had happened, and went down again quite happy.

They drew about the fire, and talked; the girls and mother working still. Bob told them of
20 the extraordinary kindness of Mr Scrooge's nephew, whom he had scarcely seen but once, and
who, meeting him in the street that day, and seeing that he looked a little – 'just a little down,
you know,' said Bob, inquired what had happened to distress him. 'On which,' said Bob, 'for he
is the pleasantest-spoken gentleman you ever heard, I told him. "I am heartily sorry for you, Mr
Cratchit." He said, "and heartily sorry for your good wife." By-the-bye, how he ever knew that I
25 don't know.'

Starting with this extract, explore how Dickens writes about the Cratchit family and their importance
in the novel.

Write about:

- how Dickens writes about the Cratchits in this extract
- how Dickens writes about the Cratchits in the novel as a whole.

[30 marks]

9 | **Charles Dickens:** *Great Expectations*

Read the following extract from Chapter 1 and then answer the question that follows.

In this extract, Pip meets Magwitch for the first time.

'Hold your noise!' cried a terrible voice, as a man started up from among the graves at the side of
the church porch. 'Keep still, you little devil, or I'll cut your throat!'

A fearful man, all in coarse gray, with a great iron on his leg. A man with no hat, and with broken
shoes, and with an old rag tied round his head. A man who had been soaked in water, and smothered in
5 mud, and lamed by stones, and cut by flints, and stung by nettles, and torn by briars; who limped, and
shivered, and glared and growled; and whose teeth chattered in his head as he seized me by the chin.

'Oh! Don't cut my throat, sir,' I pleaded in terror. 'Pray, don't do it, sir.'

'Tell us your name!' said the man. 'Quick!'

'Pip, sir.'

10 'Once more,' said the man, staring at me, 'Give it mouth!'

'Pip. Pip, sir.'

'Show us where you live,' said the man. 'Pint out the place!'

I pointed to where our village lay, on the flat inshore among the alder-trees and pollards, a
mile or more from the church.

15 The man, after looking at me for a moment, turned me upside-down, and emptied my pockets.
There was nothing in them but a piece of bread. When the church came to itself – for he was so
sudden and strong that he made it go head over heels before me, and I saw the steeple under my
feet – when the church came to itself, I say, I was seated on a high tombstone, trembling, while he
ate the bread ravenously.

20 'You young dog,' said the man, licking his lips, 'what fat cheeks you ha' got.' I believe they were
fat, though I was at that time undersized for my years, and not strong. 'Darn me if I couldn't eat
'em,' said the man, with a threatening shake of his head, 'and if I han't half a mind to't!'

Starting with this extract, write about how Dickens presents the character of Magwitch and his relationship with Pip.

Write about:

- how Dickens writes about Magwitch and the impression he makes on Pip in this extract
- how Dickens writes about Magwitch and his relationship with Pip in the novel as a whole. **[30 marks]**

10 **Charlotte Brontë:** *Jane Eyre*

Read the following extract from Chapter 17 and then answer the question that follows.

In this extract, Jane leaves the room where Mr Rochester is entertaining his friends.

> I then quitted my sheltered corner and made my exit by the side-door, which was fortunately near. Thence a narrow passage led into the hall: in crossing it, I perceived my sandal was loose; I stopped to tie it, kneeling down for that purpose on the mat at the foot of the staircase. I heard the dining-room door unclose; a gentleman came out; rising hastily, I stood face to face with him:
> 5 it was Mr Rochester. 'How do you do?' he asked.
>
> 'I am very well, sir.'
>
> 'Why did you not come and speak to me in the room?' I thought I might have retorted the question on him who put it: but I would not take that freedom. I answered –
>
> 'I did not wish to disturb you, as you seemed engaged, sir.'
>
> 10 'What have you been doing during my absence?'
>
> 'Nothing in particular; teaching Adele as usual.'
>
> 'And getting a great deal paler than you were – as I saw at first sight. What is the matter?'
>
> 'Nothing at all, sir.'
>
> 'Did you take any cold that night you half drowned me?'
>
> 15 'Not the least.'
>
> 'Return to the drawing-room: you are deserting too early.'
>
> 'I am tired, sir.'
>
> He looked at me for a minute. 'And a little depressed,' he said. 'What about? Tell me.'
>
> 'Nothing – nothing, sir. I am not depressed.'
>
> 20 'But I affirm that you are: so much depressed that a few more words would bring tears to your eyes – indeed, they are there now, shining and swimming; and a bead has slipped from the lash and fallen on the flag. If I had time, and was not in mortal dread of some prating prig of a servant passing, I would know what all this means. Well, tonight I excuse you; but understand that so long as my visitors stay, I expect you to appear in the drawing-room every evening; it is my wish; don't
> 25 neglect it. Now go, and send Sophie for Adele. Good-night, my –' He stopped, bit his lip, and abruptly left me.

Starting with this extract, explore how Brontë writes about Jane's position as a governess and her awareness of social class.

Write about:

* how Brontë writes about Jane's position as a governess in this extract
* how Brontë writes about Jane's position as a governess and her awareness of social class in the novel as a whole.   **[30 marks]**

11 **Mary Shelley: _Frankenstein_**

Read the following extract from Chapter 4 and then answer the question that follows.

In this extract, Victor Frankenstein describes his work as he begins to create the creature.

> No-one can conceive the variety of feelings which bore me onwards, like a hurricane, in the first enthusiasm of success. Life and death appeared to me ideal bounds, which I should first break through, and pour a torrent of light into our dark world. A new species would bless me as its creator and source; many happy and excellent natures would owe their being to me. No father
> 5 could claim the gratitude of his child so completely as I should deserve theirs. Pursuing these reflections, I thought that if I could bestow animation upon lifeless matter, I might in process of time (although I now found it impossible) renew life where death had apparently devoted the body to corruption.
>
> These thoughts supported my spirits, while I pursued my undertaking with unremitting ardour.
> 10 My cheek had grown pale with study, and my person had become emaciated with confinement. Sometimes, on the very brink of certainty, I failed; yet still I clung to the hope which the next day or the next hour might realize. One secret which I alone possessed was the hope to which I had dedicated myself; and the moon gazed on my midnight labours, while, with unrelaxed and breathless eagerness, I pursued nature to her hiding-places. Who shall conceive the horrors of my
> 15 secret toil as I dabbled among the unhallowed damps of the grave or tortured the living animal to animate the lifeless clay? My limbs now tremble, and my eyes swim with the remembrance; but then a resistless and almost frantic impulse urged me forward; I seemed to have lost all soul or sensation but for this one pursuit. It was indeed but a passing trance, that only made me feel with renewed acuteness so soon as, the unnatural stillness ceasing to operate, I had returned to
> 20 my old habits. I collected bones from charnel- houses and disturbed with profane fingers, the tremendous secrets of the human frame.

Starting with this extract, explore how Shelley writes about Frankenstein's feelings about his work in _Frankenstein_.

Write about:

* how Shelley writes about Frankenstein's feelings about his work in this extract
* how Shelley writes about Frankenstein's feelings about his work in the novel as a whole. **[30 marks]**

12 Jane Austen: *Pride and Prejudice*

Read the following extract from Chapter 29 (vol. 2 Chapter 6) and then answer the question that follows.

In this extract, Mr Collins expresses his delight at receiving an invitation from Lady Catherine de Burgh.

> Mr Collins's triumph in consequence of this invitation was complete. The power of displaying the grandeur of his patroness to his wondering visitors, and of letting them see her civility towards himself and his wife was exactly what he had wished for, and that an opportunity of doing it should be given so soon was an instance of Lady Catherine's condescension as he knew
> 5 not how to admire enough.
>
> 'I confess,' he said, 'that I should not have been at all surprised by her Ladyship's asking us on Sunday to drink tea and spend the evening at Rosings. I rather expected, from my knowledge of her affability, that it would happen. But who could have foreseen such an attention as this? Who could have imagined that we should receive an invitation to dinner there (an invitation moreover
> 10 including the whole party) so immediately after your arrival!'
>
> 'I am the less surprised at what has happened,' replied Sir William, 'from that knowledge of what the manners of the great really are, which my situation in life has allowed me to acquire. About the Court, such instances of elegant breeding are not uncommon.'
>
> 15 Scarcely anything was talked of the whole day or next morning, but their visit to Rosings. Mr Collins was carefully instructing them in what they were to expect, that the sight of such rooms, so many servants, and so splendid a dinner might not wholly overpower them.
>
> When the ladies were separating for the toilette, he said to Elizabeth, 'Do not make yourself uneasy, my dear cousin, about your apparel. Lady Catherine is far from requiring that elegance
> 20 of dress in us, which becomes herself and her daughter. I would advise you merely to put on whatever of your clothes is superior to the rest, there is not occasion for anything more. Lady Catherine will not think the worse of you for being simply dressed. She likes to have the distinction of rank preserved.'

Starting with this extract, explore how Austen writes about snobbery in *Pride and Prejudice*.

Write about:

- how Austen writes about snobbery in this extract
- how Austen writes about snobbery in the novel as a whole.   **[30 marks]**

13 **Sir Arthur Conan Doyle:** *The Sign of Four*

Read the following extract from Chapter 11 and then answer the question that follows.

In this extract, Watson and Miss Morstan open the box that is supposed to contain the Great Agra Treasure.

'That is all over,' I answered. 'It was nothing. I will tell you no more gloomy details. Let us turn to something brighter. There is the treasure. What could be brighter than that? I got leave to bring it with me, thinking that it would interest you to be the first to see it.'

'It would be of the greatest interest to me,' she said. There was no eagerness in her voice,
5 however. It had struck her, doubtless, that it might seem ungracious upon her part to be indifferent to a prize which had cost so much to win.

'What a pretty box!' she said, stooping over it. 'This is Indian work, I suppose?'

'Yes, it is; Benares metal-work.'

'And so heavy!' she exclaimed, trying to raise it. 'The box alone must be of some value. Where
10 is the key?'

'Small threw it into the Thames,' I answered. 'I must borrow Mrs Forrester's poker.' There was in the front a thick and broad hasp, wrought in the image of a sitting Buddha. Under this I thrust the end of the poker and twisted it outward as a lever. The hasp sprang open with a loud snap. With trembling fingers I flung back the lid. We both stood gazing in astonishment.

15 The box was empty!

No wonder that it was heavy. The iron-work was two thirds of an inch thick all round. It was massive, well made, and solid, like a chest constructed to carry things of great price, but not one shred or crumb of metal or jewellery lay within it. It was absolutely and completely empty.

'The treasure is lost,' said Miss Morstan calmly.

20 As I listened to the words and realized what they meant, a great shadow seemed to pass from my soul. I did not know how this Agra treasure had weighed me down, until now that it was finally removed. It was selfish, no doubt, disloyal, wrong, but I could realize nothing save that the golden barrier was gone from between us.

Starting with this extract, explore how Conan Doyle writes about wealth and its effect on people in *The Sign of Four*.

Write about:

- how Conan Doyle writes about the treasure in this extract
- how Conan Doyle writes about the treasure and wealth in general in the novel as a whole. **[30 marks]**

English Literature Paper 2

Modern Texts and Poetry

You should spend a total of 2 hour 15 minutes on this paper.
Answer **one** question from **Section A, one** from **Section B** and **both** questions in **Section C**.
The maximum mark for the paper is 96.
Spelling, punctuation and grammar (AO4) will be assessed in **Section A**. There are four additional marks available.

Section A: Modern Prose or Drama

Answer one question from this section on your chosen text.

J. B. Priestley: *An Inspector Calls*

EITHER

1 How does Priestley write about social problems in *An Inspector Calls*?

Write about:
- the social problems that Priestley writes about in *An Inspector Calls*
- how Priestley presents these problems by the way he writes.   **[30 marks + AO4 4 marks]**

OR

2 How does Priestley write about the role and significance of Inspector Goole in *An Inspector Calls*?

Write about:
- the role and significance of Inspector Goole
- how Priestley presents the Inspector.   **[30 marks + AO4 4 marks]**

Willy Russell: *Blood Brothers*

EITHER

3 To what extent do Mickey and his mother create their own tragedy in *Blood Brothers*?

Write about:
- what Mickey and Mrs Johnstone do and what happens to them
- how Russell writes about what they do and what happens to them.   **[30 marks + AO4 4 marks]**

OR

4 How does Russell write about the character of Linda and her relationship with Mickey and Edward in *Blood Brothers*?

Write about:
- the character of Linda and her relationship with Mickey and Edward
- how Russell presents Linda and her relationship with Mickey and Edward.   **[30 marks + AO4 4 marks]**

Alan Bennett: The History Boys

EITHER

[5] How does Bennett use the Headmaster to present ideas about education and authority in *The History Boys*?

Write about:
- what the Headmaster does and says
- how Bennett presents the Headmaster in the play.   **[30 marks + AO4 4 marks]**

OR

[6] How does Bennett write about friendships between teachers and pupils in *The History Boys*?

Write about:
- the friendships between teachers and pupils in the play
- how Bennett presents these friendships.   **[30 marks + AO4 4 marks]**

Dennis Kelly: *DNA*

EITHER

[7] How does Kelly write about the way teenagers can behave in *DNA*?

Write about:
- the actions taken by the teenage characters in *DNA*
- how Kelly presents their actions in the play.   **[30 marks + AO4 4 marks]**

OR

[8] How does Kelly present the character of Cathy as a leader in *DNA*?

Write about:
- the character of Cathy and her role as a leader
- how Kelly presents the character Cathy.   **[30 marks + AO4 4 marks]**

Simon Stephens: *The Curious Incident of the Dog in the Night-Time*

EITHER

[9] How does Stephens present Christopher as being different from other people in *The Curious Incident of the Dog in the Night-Time*?

Write about:
- things Christopher does and says that indicate his 'difference'
- how Stephens presents Christopher as being different from other characters.   **[30 marks + AO4 4 marks]**

OR

[10] 'Wellington's death causes Christopher to change in many ways.' How far do you agree with this statement?

Write about:
- to what extent Christopher changes after the death of Wellington
- how Stephens presents these changes.   **[30 marks + AO4 4 marks]**

Shelagh Delaney: *A Taste of Honey*

EITHER

11 'In *A Taste of Honey* the female characters regard the male characters as weak and unreliable.' How far do you agree with this statement?

Write about:
- how Delaney presents male characters and what they say and do
- how Helen and Jo react to and talk about men.   **[30 marks + AO4 4 marks]**

OR

12 How does Delaney write about motherhood in *A Taste of Honey*?

Write about:
- different ideas about motherhood in the play
- how Delaney presents these ideas.   **[30 marks + AO4 4 marks]**

William Golding: *Lord of the Flies*

EITHER

13 Is Simon an important character in *Lord of the Flies*?

Write about:
- the significance of Simon in *Lord of the Flies*
- how Golding presents the character of Simon.

                                                                    [30 marks + AO4 4 marks]

OR

14 How does Golding write about the idea of 'Britishness' in *Lord of the Flies*?

Write about:
- ideas about how being British is presented in the novel
- how Golding presents these ideas.   **[30 marks + AO4 4 marks]**

AQA Anthology: *Telling Tales*

EITHER

15 How do writers explore relationships between people of different generations in 'Korea' and one other story from *Telling Tales*?

Write about:
- the relationships described in the two stories
- how the writers present these relationships.   **[30 marks + AO4 4 marks]**

OR

16 How do writers explore how people change in 'The Darkness Out There' and one other story from *Telling Tales*?

Write about:
- how people change in the two stories
- how the writers present these changes.   **[30 marks + AO4 4 marks]**

George Orwell: *Animal Farm*

EITHER

17 'Orwell uses old Major and his dream to write about idealism in *Animal Farm.*' How far do you agree with this statement?

Write about:
- how Orwell presents old Major's ideals
- to what extent Orwell uses old Major's ideals to explore the results and limits of idealism.

[30 marks + AO4 4 marks]

OR

18 How does Orwell write about the pigs becoming more like humans and the other animals' reaction to this in *Animal Farm*?

Write about:
- the ways in which the pigs change and the reaction of the other animals
- how Orwell writes about these changes.

[30 marks + AO4 4 marks]

Kazuo Ishiguro: *Never Let Me Go*

EITHER

19 How does Ishiguro present Kathy and what difference does her role as narrator make to our reading of *Never Let Me Go*?

Write about:
- how Ishiguro presents Kathy's character in *Never Let Me Go*
- how she uses language as the narrator of *Never Let Me Go.*

[30 marks + AO4 4 marks]

OR

20 How does Ishiguro write about what it means to be human in *Never Let Me Go*?

Write about:
- ideas about what it means to be human presented in the novel
- how Ishiguro presents these ideas.

[30 marks + AO4 4 marks]

Meera Syal: *Anita and Me*

EITHER

21 How does Syal present Indian culture and traditions in *Anita and Me*?

Write about:
- examples of Indian culture and traditions in *Anita and Me*
- how Syal writes about Indian culture and traditions.

[30 marks + AO4 4 marks]

OR

22 How does Syal write about Meena and her family's feelings about Tollington in *Anita and Me*?

Write about:
- how Meena and her family feel about Tollington
- how Syal presents these feelings.

[30 marks + AO4 4 marks]

Stephen Kelman: *Pigeon English*

EITHER

23 How does Kelman present violence and danger in *Pigeon English*?

Write about:
- examples of violent and dangerous behaviour in *Pigeon English*
- how Kelman presents violent and dangerous behaviour. **[30 marks + AO4 4 marks]**

OR

24 How does Kelman present female characters in *Pigeon English*?

Write about:
- examples of female characters in *Pigeon English*
- how Kelman presents female characters. **[30 marks + AO4 4 marks]**

Section B: Poetry

Answer **one** question from this section.

AQA Anthology: Poems Past and Present

EITHER

Love and Relationships

25 Compare the way poets write about family relationships in 'Before You Were Mine' and one other poem from 'Love and Relationships'.

Before You Were Mine

I'm ten years away from the corner you laugh on
with your pals, Maggie McGeeney and Jean Duff.
The three of you bend from the waist, holding
each other, or your knees, and shriek at the pavement.
5   Your polka-dot dress blows round your legs. Marilyn.

I'm not here yet. The thought of me doesn't occur
in the ballroom with the thousand eyes, the fizzy, movie tomorrows
the right walk home could bring. I knew you would dance
like that. Before you were mine, your Ma stands at the close
10   with a hiding for the late one. You reckon it's worth it.

The decade ahead of my loud, possessive yell was the best one, eh?
I remember my hands in those high-heeled red shoes, relics,
and now your ghost clatters toward me over George Square
till I see you, clear as scent, under the tree,
15   with its lights, and whose small bites on your neck, sweetheart?

Cha cha cha! You'd teach me the steps on the way home from Mass,
stamping stars from the wrong pavement. Even then
I wanted the bold girl winking in Portobello, somewhere
in Scotland, before I was born. That glamorous love lasts
20   where you sparkle and waltz and laugh before you were mine.

Carol Ann Duffy

[30 marks]

OR

Power and Conflict

26   Compare the way poets write about how people are changed by experience in 'Remains' and one other poem from 'Power and Conflict'.   **[30 marks]**

Remains

On another occasion, we get sent out
to tackle looters raiding a bank.
And one of them legs it up the road,
probably armed, possibly not.

5   Well myself and somebody else and somebody else
are of the same mind,
so all three of us open fire.
Three of a kind all letting fly, and I swear

I see every round as it rips through his life –
10   I see broad daylight on the other side.
So we've hit this looter a dozen times
and he's there on the ground, sort of inside out,

pain itself, the image of agony.
One of my mates goes by
15   and tosses his guts back into his body.
Then he's carted off in the back of a lorry.

End of story, except not really.
His blood-shadow stays on the street, and out on patrol
I walk right over it week after week.
20   Then I'm home on leave. But I blink

and he bursts again through the doors of the bank.
Sleep, and he's probably armed, and possibly not.
Dream, and he's torn apart by a dozen rounds.
And the drink and the drugs won't flush him out –

25   he's here in my head when I close my eyes,
dug in deep behind enemy lines,
not left for dead in some distant, sun-stunned, sand-smothered land
or six-feet-under in desert sand,

but near to the knuckle, here and now,
30   his bloody life in my bloody hands.

Simon Armitage

Section C: Unseen Poetry

Answer **both** questions in this section.

The Darkling Thrush

I leant upon a coppice gate
  When Frost was spectre-grey,
And Winter's dregs made desolate
  The weakening eye of day.
The tangled bine-stems scored the sky
5   Like strings of broken lyres,
And all mankind that haunted nigh
  Had sought their household fires.

The land's sharp features seemed to be
  The Century's corpse outleant,
10 His crypt the cloudy canopy,
  The wind his death-lament.
The ancient pulse of germ and birth
  Was shrunken hard and dry,
And every spirit upon earth
15   Seemed fervourless as I.

At once a voice arose among
  The bleak twigs overhead
In a full-hearted evensong
  Of joy illimited;
20 An aged thrush, frail, gaunt, and small,
  In blast-beruffled plume,
Had chosen thus to fling his soul
  Upon the growing gloom.

So little cause for carolings
25   Of such ecstatic sound
Was written on terrestrial things
  Afar or nigh around,
That I could think there trembled through
  His happy good-night air
30 Some blessed Hope, whereof he knew
  And I was unaware.

Thomas Hardy

27.1 In 'The Darkling Thrush' how does the poet use natural imagery to present his mood and feelings?   **[24 marks]**

Spellbound

The night is darkening round me,
The wild winds coldly blow;
But a tyrant spell has bound me
And I cannot, cannot go.

5 The giant trees are bending
Their bare boughs weighed with snow.
And the storm is fast descending,
And yet I cannot go.

Clouds beyond clouds above me,
10 Wastes beyond wastes below;
But nothing drear can move me;
I will not, cannot go.

Emily Brontë

27.2 In both 'The Darkling Thrush' and 'Spellbound', the poets write about nature and their own feelings.

What are the similarities and/or differences between the ways the poets present nature and their feelings? **[8 marks]**

Answers

Key Technical Skills: Writing – pages 4–8

Page 4: Spelling

1. a) Is that **your** coat? **You're** in the wrong place.
    b) **They're** all in the yard eating **their** lunches, over **there** by the tree.
    c) What do you think I should **wear** for the party? **Where** did you say they **were** going?
    d) Come over **here**. I can't **hear** you very well.
    e) You have **to** choose **two** of the five options. Three would be **too** many.
    f) The cat's eaten **its** food and now **it's** asleep.
        [1] for each correct answer up to a maximum of **[15]**
2. If you are going to improve your **performance** in any area, **whether** in a sport, a hobby or in **your studies**, you must **practise**. **Successful** people who have **achieved** great things in life always say it is **because** of hard work just as much as talent. You **might** not want to be an Olympic champion, but you can still get a lot of satisfaction from **knowing** you have improved.
        [1] for each correct answer up to a maximum of **[10]**
3. a) tornadoes
    b) women
    c) antibodies
    d) antitheses
    e) soliloquys   **[maximum 5]**

Page 5: Punctuation

1. *Anita and Me* is a novel based on the author's own childhood. **[1]** It is the story of a family who come from India. **[1]** They settle in a village in the English Midlands. **[1]** The narrator makes friends with a girl called Anita. **[1]** Their friendship is the focus of the book. **[1]**   **[maximum 5]**
2. *Pride and Prejudice* is Jane Austen's **[1]** most popular book. Elizabeth, **[1]** one of five sisters, **[1]** meets a man called Mr Darcy, **[1]** who is very rich and rather snobbish. Darcy's **[1]** best friend, **[1]** whose name is Mr Bingley, **[1]** falls in love with Elizabeth's **[1]** older sister. The sisters' **[1]** relationships don't **[1]** go smoothly.   **[maximum 10]**
3. a) Where did they come from? Nobody knows.
    b) What a lovely surprise! It was just what I wanted.
    c) Pip (the hero of the story) meets Magwitch on the marshes.
    d) Kai had rice pudding; Ellie chose the cheese.
    e) We love Birmingham: it has everything a city should have.
        [1] for each correct answer up to a maximum of **[5]**

Page 6: Sentence Structure

1. a) Jo lives next door to me **and** Mo lives next door to her. **[1]**
    b) Mo has a dog **but** Jo does not have any pets. **[1]**
2. a) **Although** he worked as quickly as he could, he did not finish on time. **[1]**
    b) I missed the bus **because** I stopped to talk to someone on the way. **[1]**
3. Tom, **who** is my best friend, lives on the main road. **[1]**
4. a) simple   b) compound   c) minor
    d) complex   e) complex
        [1] for each correct answer up to a maximum of **[5]**

Page 7: Text Structure and Organisation

1. b), d), a), e), c)   **[maximum 5]**
2. a) After   b) Despite   c) however   d) therefore
    e) Nevertheless   **[maximum 5]**

Page 8: Standard English and Grammar

1. a) are b) are c) were d) did e) has been
    f) have done g) were; had done   **[maximum 8]**

2. a) got; invitations   b) few; broken   **[maximum 4]**
3. I was **standing** in the street minding **my** own business when I **saw** Zaki. **[1]** He **came** over to me acting **very (or really) casual**. **[1]** Zaki **and I** were best mates (*or* **friends**). **[1]** I was **going to** ask him how he **did** (*or* **had done**) in his exams. **[1]** I **did not say anything** though. **[1]** I could see he **had done well**. **[1]** Then I **noticed** (*or* **saw**) Kirsty **sitting** on the wall. **[1]** 'Did you (*or* **you two**) **fail** your exams again?' she shouted. **[1]**
        [1] for each sentence re-written in correct Standard English up to a maximum of **[8]**

Key Technical Skills: Reading – pages 9–16

Page 9: Explicit Information and Ideas

1. a) ✓ c) ✓ e) ✓ h) ✓   **[maximum 4]**
2. **Any four from:** He was very nice looking. He had a fresh-coloured face. He was clean shaven. He had white hair. He wore oddly shaped collars. He wore a top hat.   **[maximum 4]**

Page 10: Implicit Information and Ideas

1. a) B b) A c) C d) C e) B f) A
    g) C h) A   **[maximum 8]**
2. a) ✓ b) ✓ e) ✓ g) ✓   **[maximum 4]**

Page 11: Synthesis and Summary 1

1. a) Jackie won the sack race. b) Give me the letter now.
    c) Wind blew over two trees.   **[maximum 3]**
2. a) ✓ d) ✓ e) ✓ f) ✓ h) ✓   **[maximum 5]**
3. The summary below is a suggestion only. You should have included details of what exactly happened (the tree being blown onto the car) and when and where it happened. When I left number 5 Roland Street **[1]**, at four o'clock **[1]**, it was very windy **[1]**. A car **[1]** came round the corner **[1]** from Bilton Road **[1]**. Just then, a tree **[1]** was blown over **[1]** and landed across its bonnet **[1]**. The driver braked suddenly **[1]**. Two people got out of the car **[1]** unhurt **[1]**.   **[maximum 12]**

Page 12: Synthesis and Summary 2

1.

Similarities	Differences
They are both about roads.	The road in A is a private road and JDS does not know who owns it, but the one in B is the responsibility of the council.
They both think the state of the roads are poor.	B talks about parking while A is only about the state of the road.
They both mention the fact that they are paying for the roads.	JDS mentions part of the road being in 'excellent repair'. Amina comments on all of the road being bad.
They both want something done about the roads.	JDS wants an 'inquiry'. Amina wants action from the council.
	The road in B is in a 'busy town centre' but the one in A appears not to be, as it is 'approaching Garston'.
	Amina lives and has a shop on the road; JDS does not live there (he complains that residents do not have to pay).

[1] for each similarity or difference pointed out up to a maximum of **[10]**.
2. Look at the mark scheme below, decide which description is closest to your answer and decide what mark to give it up to a maximum of **[8]**.

Marks	Skills
7–8	You have given a perceptive interpretation of both texts. You have synthethised evidence from the texts. You have used appropriate quotations from both texts.
5–6	You have started to interpret both texts. You have shown clear connections between the texts. You have used relevant quotations from both texts.

Page 13: Referring to the Text

1. a)–y); b)–z); c)–x)   **[maximum 3]**
2. a) Romeo refers to Juliet as a 'bright angel'. **[2]**
   b) Romeo rejects his family: 'Henceforth I never will be Romeo.' **[2]**
   c) When Juliet asks how he found her, Romeo replies:
      By love, that first did prompt me to enquire.
      He lent me counsel, and I lent him eyes. **[2]**
3. a) Gratiano insults Shylock, **[P]** calling him 'an inexecrable dog', **[E]** a metaphor that implies that he considers Shylock less than human. **[Ex] [3]**
   b) By the end of the novel, Scrooge is a reformed character, **[P]** shown by his gift of the turkey to the Cratchits, **[E]** a generous gesture that the old Scrooge would never have made. **[Ex] [3]**.

Page 14: Analysing Language 1

1. a) kingdom – noun   b) dominant – adjective
   c) the – determiner   d) or – conjunction
   e) accidentally – adverb   f) brought – verb
   g) with – preposition   h) them – pronoun   **[maximum 8]**
2. a) Mars   b) complex   c) which   d) active   **[maximum 4]**
3. a) Formal and technical   **[maximum 2]**
   b) Up to **[2]** marks for each reasonable explanation, e.g. 'The language is associated with science and reads like an explanation in a school text book' and 'It is written in Standard English'.   **[maximum 4]**

Page 15: Analysing Language 2

1. a) alliteration – great grinning giant's
   b) personification – looked danger in the face
   c) onomatopoeia – squelched   **[maximum 3]**
2.

She came into the room like a tornado.	simile	A tornado is a strong wind. The comparison implies she entered suddenly and quickly and might have been frightening. (Or a similar explanation.)
You are my rock.	metaphor	The person addressed is seen as strong and solid like a rock, implying reliability. (Or a similar explanation.)

   [maximum 4]

3. Look at the mark scheme below, decide which description best fits your answer and decide what mark to give it up to a maximum of **[8]**

Marks	Skills Examples of possible content
7–8	**Skills** • You have analysed the effects of the writer's choice of language. • You have used an appropriate range of quotations. • You have used sophisticated subject terminology appropriately.

	Example of possible content In the first sentence the narrator uses three adjectives to build a picture of an unpleasant winter's day: 'bleak', 'hard' and 'black'. This literal imagery can be viewed as a simple description of the environment and its physical effect on the narrator, making him 'shiver through every limb' but readers might see it as pathetic fallacy, reflecting the coldness of the welcome he is about to receive. The narrator reacts to being locked out with a spurt of physical activity as he jumps over the chained gate and runs up the path. However, his positivity is not reflected in what he sees – the chain clearly showing that visitors are unwelcome, 'straggling gooseberry bushes' indicating neglect. After describing what he can see (though he does not seem to get the message) he turns to the sound coming from the house: 'the dogs howled'. The onomatopoeic 'howled' vividly conveys both neglect and hostility.
5–6	**Skills** • You have clearly explained the effects of the writer's choice of language. • You have used a range of relevant quotations. • You have used subject terminology appropriately. **Example of possible content** The writer uses the adjectives 'bleak', 'hard' and 'black' to show how cold and unfriendly the place is. The narrator shivers 'through every limb'. The verbs 'jumped' and 'running' show that the narrator is very active and is not easily put off by the bad weather or the chain that is keeping him out. The 'straggling gooseberry bushes' show neglect. His hands are 'tingling', which again emphasises how cold he feels. This reflects the metaphorically cold unfriendliness of the house.

Page 16: Analysing Form and Structure

1. a)–z); b)–x); c)–y)   **[maximum 3]**
2. a) A church service   b) It is winter/it takes place near the sea.   c) It creates a gloomy/mysterious atmosphere.   d) The silence might lead to a feeling that something is about to break it/The storminess of the sea creates an atmosphere of danger.   e) The important thing about them is their jobs/The writer is deliberately holding back the information.   f) Any reasonable answer mentioning the sailor and what he is doing there. Up to **[2]** marks for each answer to a maximum of **[12]**

English Language 1 – pages 17–20

Page 17: Creative Reading 1

1. a) D (also accept B)   b) C   c) B   d) A   **[maximum 4]**

Page 18: Creative Reading 2

1. **[1]** for each correct answer in the second column and up to **[2]** for each answer similar to those given in column 3.

Character	How we learn about the character	What we learn about the character
Lady Catherine de Burgh	Narrator's description	She is snobbish, domineering/intimidating.
Mary Morstan	How others react to the character	She is attractive/perhaps concerned about the narrator/The narrator is in love with her.

Mrs Fairfax	What the character does	She is kind-hearted/caring/practical.
Fezziwig	What the character says	He is in charge/He is generous/He enjoys himself/He is outgoing.
Hyde	What others say to/about the character	There is something odd and mysterious about him, almost inhuman.

Page 19: Narrative Writing

The following are examples of the sort of thing you might write. Your answers are likely to be completely different.
1. a) First
   b) No
   c) i) Male ii) Impossible to tell
      iii) Green, antennae, one large eye
      iv) From outer space v) Has a pet
   d) An ordinary street in England.
   e) Next year
   f) A year
   [1] for each reasonable answer up to a maximum of [10].
2. a) My family and our street. b) A new neighbour arrives. c) We find out he is from Mars and wants to return but his spaceship is lost. d) We find the spaceship and he goes home. e) Life is almost back to normal but we're expecting another new neighbour. [2] for each reasonable answer up to a maximum of [10]

Page 20: Descriptive Writing

These answers are examples only. Your answers are likely to be completely different.
1. a) Third [1] b) Past [1] c) i) A narrow Victorian street in town. [2] ii) A neat house with flowers in the window boxes. [2] iii) The fire in the back room. [2]
2. a) Flickering flames [2] b) Crackling logs [2] c) Freshly baked bread [2] d) Raspberry jam [2] e) Soft cushions [2]
3. a) As welcoming as a warm hug. [1] b) The house was an enchanted castle. [1]

English Language 2 – pages 21–22

Page 21: Reading Non-fiction

Up to [2] for each answer similar to the following, to a maximum of [20]

	Text A	Text B
What is the text about?	Staying at a hotel/guest house called Holcombe Manor.	Staying at a hotel/guest house called Holcombe Manor.
What is the writer's attitude to Holcombe Manor?	Felt 'at home'. Thought it was welcoming and cosy. Enthusiastic about hosts. Enjoyed the stay.	Thought it was cut off, cramped and unclean. Disliked host. Did not enjoy the stay.
What impression do you get of the writer?	Likes peace and quiet. Interested in history.	Likes modern facilities. Might be prejudiced against 'posh' people. High standards or a bit intolerant?
How would you describe the general tone and style?	Enthusiastic/positive.	Negative/insulting.
Comment on any interesting language features.	Uses a lot of positive but quite clichéd adjectives. Fairly formal tone.	Starts by addressing readers. Colloquial tone.

Page 22: Writing Non-fiction

The following are only suggestions. There are many other points you could make. [1] for each up to as maximum of [10]

For	Against
There are many examples of people who are successful without qualifications.	There are different types of success and fame/celebrity culture is shallow.
'Instant' success on reality shows can lead to other opportunities ordinary people don't often get.	Instant success can lead to great stress, unhappiness and mental health issues.
You could work really hard and even be successful academically but still not be well-paid or happy.	Academic work is not just about success. It broadens the mind and is interesting in itself.
The sort of work you do in school does not always help you afterwards.	Even if you gain fame and fortune easily, it's a good idea to have a 'back up' in case things go wrong.
Reality shows are too easily dismissed. Many who appear on them have worked hard and are still working hard to achieve their ambitions.	The two things are not mutually exclusive.

2. [1] for each of the following up to a maximum of [5].
   - Opening with 'Dear Sir/Madam/Editor'.
   - Setting out the opening correctly.
   - Using a formal tone.
   - Clearly stating the purpose of your letter.
   - Presenting your point of view clearly.
   - Using a literary or rhetorical device.
   - Accurate punctuation and spelling.
3. [1] for each of the following up to a maximum of [5]
   - Using an intriguing or amusing headline.
   - Using a strapline.
   - Using an appropriate informal tone.
   - Clearly stating the purpose of your article.
   - Presenting your point of view clearly.
   - Using a literary or rhetorical device.
   - Accurate punctuation and spelling.

Shakespeare – pages 23–24

Page 23: Context and Themes

1. Up to [2] for each reasonable answer up to a maximum of [10]
2. Up to [2] for each reasonable answer up to a maximum of [10]

Page 24: Characters, Language and Structure

1. [2] for each quotation and [2] for a reasonable interpretation up to a maximum of [8]
2. [1] for each correct answer and [2] for a reasonable explanation similar to the suggestions below up to a maximum of [12]
   a) Rhetorical question. The speaker expresses outrage and disbelief at the suggestion that he thinks had been made, answering the question in the negative.
   b) Oxymoron. Its use suggests both Romeo's confusion about love and how themes of love and hate are intertwined in the play.
   c) Metaphor. By comparing oaths to straw that could be destroyed by fire, the speaker emphasises how weak and worthless they are.
   d) Simile. The Captain expresses how much stronger than their enemies Banquo and Macbeth are by comparing them to powerful animals and their enemies to their prey.

The 19th-Century Novel – pages 25–26

Page 25: Context and Themes

1. a) **[1]** for each reasonable answer up to a maximum of **[5]**
   b) Up to **[2]** for each reasonable answer up to a maximum of **[10]**
2. Up to **[2]** for each reasonable answer up to a maximum of **[10]**

Page 26: Character, Language and Structure

1. **[1]** for every box completed with a reasonable answer for each character up to a maximum of **[25]**
2. a)–y), b)–v), c)–z), d)–w), e)–x) **[5]**

Modern Texts – pages 27–28

Page 27: Context and Themes

1. Check your answers against the text you have studied and give yourself **[1]** mark for each correct answer up to a maximum of **[5]**
2. Below are examples of the kind of answer that you might have given. Give yourself up to **[5]** marks for each reasonable answer similar to these, depending on how full your answer is.
   a) *An inspector Calls* is set shortly before the First World War, in 1912, in a 'large city' in the Midlands. The family is middle-class and wealthy, Mr Birling being a self-made man who has married someone from a higher social class. They are 'comfortable' and smug, but the Inspector reveals the dark side of their world.
   b) The world of *Never Let Me Go* seems to be just like the real world of just a few years ago, However, there are aspects of this world which are not real. Breeding people to provide spare parts is not something that is done officially now, although there are cases of people having children to provide genetic material for existing children who are sick.
3. **[1]** for each theme up to a maximum of **[3]**. Up to **[2]** for each reasonable explanation up to a maximum of **[6]**.

Page 28: Characters, Language and Structure

1. **[1]** for each appropriate answer up to a maximum of **[5]**
2. **[1]** for every box completed with a reasonable answer for each character up to a maximum of **[25]**

Poetry – pages 29–31

Page 29: Context and Themes

1. a)–w), b)–x), c)–v), d)–z), e)–y) **[maximum 5]**
2. a)–w), b)–z), c)–v), d)–y), e)–x) **[maximum 5]**
3. The following answers are suggestions. You may have listed other poems.
   a) 'Eden Rock', 'The Farmer's Bride', 'Singh Song!', 'Winter Swans'.
   b) 'Eden Rock', 'Follower', 'Walking Away', 'Before You Were Mine', 'Mother, any distance'.
   c) 'When We Two Parted', 'Neutral Tones', Singh Song!', 'Love's Philosophy', Sonnet 29, 'Winter Swans'.
   d) 'The Farmer's Bride', 'Letters From Yorkshire', 'Winter Swans' ,'Follower', 'Love's Philosophy', 'Neutral Tones'.
   e) 'Eden Rock', 'Porphyria's Lover', Sonnet 29, 'When We Two Parted'. **[maximum 15]**
4. The following answers are suggestions. You may have listed other poems.
   a) ''The Charge of the Light Brigade', 'Exposure', 'Bayonet Charge', 'Remains', 'Poppies'.
   b) 'Poppies', 'War Photographer', 'The Emigree', 'Kamikaze'.

   c) 'Ozymandias', 'London', 'My Last Duchess', 'Checking Out Me History', 'The Charge of the Light Brigade'.
   d) 'Checking Out Me History', 'The Emigree', 'Poppies', 'Remains', Extract from 'The Prelude', 'Kamikaze'.
   e) Extract from 'The Prelude', 'Bayonet Charge', 'Kamikaze', 'Poppies'. **[maximum 15]**

Page 30: Language, Form and Structure

1. a) Sonnet 29 b) 'Neutral Tones' c) 'The Farmer's Bride' d) 'Follower' **[4]**
2. a) Extract from 'The Prelude'/'My Last Duchess'/'Checking Out Me History' b) 'London' c) 'My Last Duchess' d) 'The Charge of the Light Brigade'/'Exposure' **[4]**
3. a) Alliteration and pathetic fallacy. The alliteration of 'l' and 's' (also called sibilance) helps to make the line sound gentle and sad. The image of the earth starving adds to the sense of bleakness and despair.
   b) Metaphor. The metaphors give a picture of the nature of the relationship. The poet is flying away but his mother is holding him to the ground.
   c) Repetition and archaic language. The repetition of 'long' increases the sense of the future stretching ahead. The archaic language perhaps makes it sound more important, almost religious.
   d) Onomatopoeia. 'Clatters' creates a vivid picture through sound of the poet's mother walking along the pavement. **[maximum 16]**
4. a) Simile. By comparing the soldier's foot to a statue, the poet creates a sense of him being frozen in time, emphasising the importance of the moment.
   b) Assonance and simile. The repetition of the long 'o' gives a sense of calm regularity. The comparison to a swan gives a sense that the poet and his boat are part of nature.
   c) Dialect and repetition. The use of dialect gives a sense of the speaker's heritage and identity. Repetition emphasises his point, highlighting how 'dem' are different from the poet but are in charge.
   d) Pathetic fallacy. The poet creates mood and atmosphere by giving human feelings to the wind and trees. **[maximum 16]**

Pages 31–32: Unseen Poetry

1. **[1]** for each answer similar to those given below up to a maximum of **[10]**. Other answers might be equally valid.
   a) The poet or speaker's birthday.
   b) The poet or speaker celebrating being in love and how her life has changed.
   c) Yes. Two stanzas, each of which contains two quatrains. Each line has four stressed syllables. Each quatrain rhymes *abcb* but the final line ends in a half-rhyme. The regularity contains the poet's emotions. The change in the final line gives a strong ending on 'me'.
   d) The heart is a common symbol for love or emotion.
   e) It creates a strong focus on the poet's emotional state as she tries to explain it in a series of images.
   f) A singing bird, an apple tree, a shell. They are all beautiful, natural things.
   g) A sense of beauty, richness and luxury.
   h) 'Raise', 'carve' and 'work'. They make the poet seem in command, like a queen giving orders.
   i) Happy, elated, excited, joyful, looking forward to her future.
   j) The arrival of her love is like a new birthday, signifying that her life is about to change forever.
2. The answers below are suggestions. There may be other valid responses. Up to **[2]** for every box completed with a valid answer up to a maximum of **[36]**

	A Birthday	On His Eightieth Birthday
Speaker or voice	A person, possibly the poet, who has fallen in love.	An old man, probably the poet.
Structure	Two stanzas of eight lines (octaves).	One stanza of four lines (quatrain).
Rhythm/metre	Tetrameter, with variation in stress.	Iambic pentameter.
Rhyme	Regular until final line, which is a half-rhyme.	*Abab* – regular with no variation.
Vocabulary/register	Formal but personal using language of nature and riches. Second stanza in second person.	Formal but personal.
Use of sound	Repetition. Brief alliteration ('because...birthday').	Alliteration in 'steps...steady' and 'where... would'.
Imagery	Series of similes taken from nature, followed by a series of images of richness and luxury.	Literal imagery describing the past. Personification of 'Death'.
Themes	Celebration of being in love. The future.	Old age. Memories of love. The past. Death.
The poet's attitude	Positive and joyful. Excited – perhaps a bit self-centred.	Thoughtful/melancholy. Content.

Practice Exam Papers – pages 33–58

Page 33 English Language Paper 1 – Section A: Reading

1. Any four from:
   - He came from Calcutta.
   - He felt like a fish out of water.
   - He lived and worked in a shed.
   - His salary was small.
   - He cooked his own meals.
   - He shared his meals with Ratan.
   - Ratan did odd jobs for him.

   [1] for each up to a maximum of [4]

2. Look at the mark scheme below, decide which description is closest to your answer and then decide what mark to give it up to a maximum of [8].

Marks	Skills	Examples of possible content
7–8	• You have analysed the effects of the choice of language. • You have chosen an appropriate range of examples. • You have used a range of subject terminology appropriately.	The paragraph consists of one complex sentence, in which the writer uses details of sights, sounds and the feelings they invoke to build a picture of life in an Indian village. 'The village cowsheds' give a sense of ordinary everyday life in contrast with the natural sound of the cicadas and the mysterious spiritual song of the Baül sect, its harshness reflected in the alliteration of 'sect sang their shrill songs'. A sense of mystery, almost fear, is created in 'ghostly shiver' running down the back of the imagined poet before the writer brings us down to earth with the alliterative but prosaic image of the postmaster lighting his 'little lamp', the size of the lamp reflecting his own insignificance.
5–6	• You have clearly explained the effects of the choice of language. • You have chosen relevant examples. • You have used subject terminology appropriately.	The paragraph is one long sentence, describing the sights and sounds of the village. The alliteration in 'cicadas chirping' and 'sang their shrill songs' brings the noises to life and makes them sound a bit frightening. The poet feels a 'shiver' in his back. At the end we focus on the postmaster. His 'little lamp' describes his own smallness in the forest.

3. Look at the mark scheme below, decide which description is closest to your answer and then decide what mark to give it up to a maximum of [8].

Marks	Skills	Examples of possible content
7–8	• You have analysed the use of structural features. • You have chosen an appropriate range of examples. • You have used a range of subject terminology appropriately.	The extract starts with a very brief description of the protagonist and how he fits into the village. The third paragraph focuses on the sights and sounds of the village to build an atmosphere and give a sense of the postmaster's environment. A new character, Ratan, is introduced and the writer uses the modal verb 'would' to introduce an account of their routine. A short passage of dialogue gives a sense of their relationship as the focus shifts to Ratan and her background is filled in through what she tells the postmaster. Then the focus shifts from general exposition to a particular time ('one noon') and back to the protagonist and his loneliness. The final paragraph describes a turning point in their relationship as he offers to teach Ratan to read, making the reader wonder what difference this might make to them and their relationship.
5–6	• You have clearly explained the effects of structural features. • You have chosen relevant examples. • You have used subject terminology appropriately.	The extract starts by telling us where the protagonist comes from and who he is. It then describes the village where he lives. Focus moves to Ratan, and we are told about how she and the postmaster interact. The phrase 'one noon' marks the beginning of the story after the exposition. We learn that the postmaster is lonely. In the final paragraph, he offers to teach Ratan to read and we wonder where this will lead for both of them.

4. Look at the mark scheme below, decide which description is closest to your answer and then decide what mark to give it up to a maximum of **[20]**.

Marks	Skills	Examples of possible content
16–20	• You have critically evaluated the text in a detailed way. • You have used examples from the text to explain your views convincingly. • You have analysed a range of the writer's methods. • You have developed a convincing response to the focus of the statement.	The immediate impression given of the postmaster is of someone alone in an unfamiliar place, emphasised by the common simile 'like a fish out of water' and the literal imagery of the slimy pond and ramshackle house, which give the impression of an unwelcoming environment. His only friend is also alone in the world, but she is very different from him and their relationship is not equal. She calls him 'sir' and does 'odd jobs' for him. However, as they talk to each other about their past they become closer. Ratan chooses to remember happy times rather than 'greater things', which the reader might infer are sad or even tragic. The postmaster's own memories are described as 'haunting', the adjective with its connotations of the supernatural, suggesting mystery and sadness. The postmaster is still lonely, however, his mood beautifully evoked by the image of the bird and the 'murmuring leaves' expressing his feelings for him. His response to his need for companionship is to draw closer to Ratan. He starts to teach her to read, showing that she is a lot more to him than a servant. She calls him 'Dada', suggesting he has now replaced her lost family.
11–15	• You have clearly evaluated the text. • You have used examples from the text to explain your views clearly. • You have clearly explained the effect of the writer's methods. • You have made a clear and relevant response to the focus of the statement.	The postmaster is described in a simile as 'like a fish out of water'. He has come from Calcutta and does not know anyone so is very lonely. Ratan is also on her own. She is an 'orphan girl' who helps him out doing 'odd jobs'. At first, she is like a servant to him but they get to know each other and talk about their past lives. The postmaster's memories are 'haunting' him which makes him seem sad and the reader feel sorry for him. The writer uses pathetic fallacy to show his mood. He thinks the birds and the leaves are talking about his loneliness. He wants a special person to share his life with. He becomes closer to Ratan and she thinks of him as her family. They have not got much in common, but their friendship is touching and they are both less lonely.

Section B: Writing

5. Look at the mark scheme below, decide which description is closest to your answer and then decide which mark to give yourself. This task is marked for content and organisation, and for technical accuracy.

Content and Organisation [maximum 24]:

22–24	**Content** • You have communicated convincingly and compellingly throughout. • Your tone, style and register assuredly match purpose, form and audience. • You have used an extensive and ambitious vocabulary with sustained crafting of linguistic devices. **Organisation** • Your writing is highly structured and developed, including a range of integrated and complex ideas. • Your paragraphs are fluently linked with integrated discourse markers. • You have used a variety of structural features in an inventive way.
19–21	**Content** • You have communicated convincingly. • Your tone, style and register consistently match purpose, form and audience. • You have used an increasingly sophisticated vocabulary with a range of appropriate linguistic devices. **Organisation** • Your writing is structured and developed, including a range of engaging ideas. • You have used paragraphs consistently with integrated discourse markers. • You have used a variety of structural features effectively.
16–18	**Content** • You have communicated clearly and effectively. • Your tone, style and register match purpose, form and audience. • You have used an extensive vocabulary with a range of linguistic devices. **Organisation** • Your writing is engaging, including a range of detailed, connected ideas. • You have used paragraphs coherently with integrated discourse markers. • You have used structural features effectively.
13–15	**Content** • You have communicated clearly. • Your tone, style and register generally match purpose, form and audience. • You have used vocabulary for effect with a range of linguistic devices. **Organisation** • Your writing is engaging, including a range of connected ideas. • You have used paragraphs coherently with a range of discourse markers. • You have usually used structural features effectively.

Technical Accuracy [maximum 16]:

13–16	• You have consistently demarcated sentences accurately. • You have used a wide range of punctuation with a high level of accuracy. • You have used a full range of sentence forms for effect. • You have used Standard English consistently and accurately, with secure control of grammatical structures. • You have achieved a high level of accuracy in spelling, including ambitious vocabulary. • Your use of vocabulary is extensive and ambitious.
9–12	• You have usually demarcated sentences accurately. • You have used a range of punctuation, usually accurately. • You have used a variety of sentence forms for effect. • You have used Standard English appropriately with control of grammatical structures. • You have spelled most words, including complex words, correctly. • Your use of vocabulary is increasingly sophisticated.

Page 36 English Language Paper 2 – Section A: Reading

1. B C F G **[maximum 4]**
2. Look at the mark scheme below, decide which description is closest to your answer and then decide what mark to give it up to a maximum of **[8]**.

Marks	Skills	Examples of possible content
7–8	• You have given a perceptive interpretation of both texts. • You have synthesised evidence from the texts. • You have used appropriate quotations from both texts.	Both writers describe behaviour they consider to be 'familiarity' (Trollope) or 'over-familiarity' (Boyle). The former criticises the behaviour of a particular neighbour before talking about Americans in general, while the latter mentions waiters, TV presenters and teachers. Trollope acknowledges the woman is helpful and intends to be friendly, and concludes her 'violent intimacy' is the norm in the USA. Boyle does not think the behaviour he describes is genuine and thinks it is copied from an idea of American friendliness. Both are concerned with forms of address. Trollope says that she and her husband are called 'the old man' and 'the English old woman' while ordinary working people such as 'draymen, butchers' boys and labourers' are referred to as 'them gentlemen'. Boyle is concerned with service rather than class and says staff in restaurants in France and Italy behave properly in contrast with those serving in Britain.
5–6	• You have started to interpret both texts. • You have shown clear connections between the texts. • You have used relevant quotations from both texts.	Trollope writes about the manners of Americans, Boyle about British people who imitate American manners. The behaviour Trollope describes is mostly from a woman who is over friendly, using first names and calling the children 'honey'. Boyle writes mostly about waiters. He says they now say, 'You guys' instead of 'Sir/Madam'. He says others, like teachers, do the same thing.

3. Look at the mark scheme below, decide which description is closest to your answer and then decide what mark to give it up to a maximum of **[12]**.

Marks	Skills	Examples of possible content
10–12	• You have analysed the effects of the choice of language. • You have used an appropriate range of quotations. • You have used sophisticated subject terminology appropriately.	Trollope starts with an anecdote to illustrate her point. She describes the situation in an understated, undramatic way ('absent rather longer than we expected') so it is clear that the search is not in itself the point of the story. Her later use of hyperbole, for example, 'exceedingly coarse and vehement' and 'violent intimacy', and the idea that the woman 'almost frightened' her (when you might think she'd be more frightened about her children being missing) suggests she wants to both shock and amuse, as does her reference to the 'amusement' of her children. In the second paragraph she uses a lot of direct speech to give the reader a flavour of American manners. She quotes the dialect of the Americans: 'That there lady… what is making dip-candles'. Here both the juxtaposition of the term 'lady' (in England usually someone who did not work) and 'making dip-candles' and the use of the non-standard 'that there' and 'what is' add both to the vividness of the picture and its humorous tone. Yet the tone seems affectionate, with a hint of self-deprecation, so you do not feel that she is 'making fun' of her neighbours.
7–9	• You have clearly explained the effects of the choice of language. • You have used a range of relevant quotations. • You have used subject terminology appropriately.	The narrative is formal, with long sentences and formal, old-fashioned Standard English: 'our party determined' and 'such a pair had been seen to pass'. When she meets the woman whom she compares to a market woman to give readers an idea of her appearance, her language becomes more dramatic. The woman is 'coarse and vehement' and Trollope does not like her 'violent intimacy'. She wants to put across how Americans speak so she uses a lot of quotations in the second half. Phrases like 'them gentlemen' and 'that there lady' convey both their dialect and their attitude.

4. Look at the mark scheme below, decide which description is closest to your answer and then decide what mark to give it up to a maximum of **[16]**.

Marks	Skills	Examples of possible content
13–16	• You have compared ideas and perspectives in a perceptive way. • You have analysed methods used to convey ideas and perspectives. • You have used a range of appropriate quotations.	The two writers have broadly similar attitudes to manners. They both prefer a degree of formality. Trollope uses the word 'familiarity' and Boyle 'over–familiarity' in the same pejorative way. Trollope is shocked ('almost frightened') by some of the ways of Americans while Boyle is 'outraged' by being addressed in a familiar, American-style way by a waiter. However, Trollope's purpose in writing is to inform her audience of the ways of Americans, remarking that such manners are 'universal' in the USA, while Boyle assumes his audience is familiar with the behaviour he is complaining about. He is putting forward an argument about the Americanisation of manners in Britain and expressing his distaste. Consequently, his tone is one of comic exaggerated outrage ('I would never leave the house'; 'never, ever') mixed with a serious attempt to analyse what he sees. Trollope too uses comedy but she is concerned more with reporting what she sees than analysis.
9–12	• You have compared ideas and perspectives in a clear and relevant way. • You have explained clearly methods used to convey ideas and perspectives. • You have used relevant quotations from both texts.	The two writers both dislike 'familiarity' and get upset by people being too informal with them. However, in Boyle's case he is only talking about staff in restaurants while Trollope is talking about Americans in general. Trollope is writing a book about the 'manners' of Americans so we can infer that at that time people in England behaved in a very different way. Boyle's main complaint is that phrases like 'you guys' have been 'imported from America'. He wants us to be different from them. They both use quotations in order to criticise them and amuse the reader: 'them gentlemen' and 'Listen up, guys'. Boyle is angrier than Trollope, who is just surprised by what she hears.

Section B: Writing

5. Look at the mark scheme for question 5 on page 64, decide which description is closest to your answer and then decide which mark to give yourself up to a maximum of **[40]**. The task is marked for content and organisation, and for technical accuracy.

Page 39 English Literature Paper 1 – Shakespeare and the 19th-Century Novel

Section A: Shakespeare

For all questions, look at the mark scheme below, decide which description is closest to your answer and then decide which mark to give yourself up to a maximum of **[30]**.

Marks	Skills
26–30	• You have responded to the task in an exploratory and critical way. • You have used precise, appropriate references to support your interpretation. • You have analysed the writer's methods using subject terminology appropriately. • You have explored the effects of the writer's methods. • You have explored links between text and ideas/context.
21–25	• You have responded to the task in a thoughtful, developed way. • You have used appropriate references to support your interpretation. • You have examined the writer's methods using subject terminology appropriately. • You have examined the effects of the writer's methods. • You have thoughtfully considered links between text and ideas/context.
16–20	• You have responded to the task in a clear way. • You have used references effectively to support your explanation. • You have clearly explained the writer's methods, using relevant subject terminology. • You have understood the effects of the writer's methods. • You have clearly understood links between text and ideas/context.

This question is also marked for AO4 (spelling, punctuation and grammar) up to a maximum of **[4]**.

Marks	Skills
4	• You have spelled and punctuated with consistent accuracy. • You have consistently used vocabulary and sentence structure to achieve effective control of meaning.
2–3	• You have spelled and punctuated with considerable accuracy. • You have consistently used a considerable range of vocabulary and sentence structure to achieve general control of meaning.

Your answers could include some of the following points.

1. **Macbeth**
   - Macduff's speech is broken up by caesuras.
   - He asks a series of short questions, seeming not to believe the news.
   - He accepts Malcolm's advice but asserts he must 'feel it as a man'.
   - The scene gives Macduff the personal motivation to seek revenge.
   - He gains sympathy as a family man and for showing his feelings.
   - Earlier he passed Malcolm's 'test' by showing his own integrity.
   - He is seen as loyal and brave, as Macbeth was at the start of the play.
   - He fights bravely and fiercely, and is patriotic and loyal to Malcolm.
   - Unlike Macbeth, he is honest and neither cruel nor ambitious.
   - When he kills Macbeth we learn he was 'from his mother's womb/Untimely ripped', so the witches' prophecy can be true.

2. **Romeo and Juliet**
   - Friar Laurence is surprised and shocked by Romeo saying he loves Juliet.
   - He sees Romeo (and all young men) as fickle, their love 'not truly in their hearts, but in their eyes'.
   - He recalls how love for Rosaline made Romeo miserable.
   - He distinguishes between 'doting' and 'loving', not believing Romeo truly loved Rosaline.
   - Juliet returns Romeo's love – 'Doth grace for grace and love for love allow'.
   - Friar Laurence might not be convinced but sees an opportunity for reconciling the Capulets and Montagues.
   - Romeo and Juliet's love is seen as strong and mutual when they meet.
   - Love is also complete when they marry, giving spiritual and sexual fulfilment.
   - However, it puts them in opposition to their families, leading to their deaths.

3. **The Tempest**
   - Caliban does not seem to want freedom, just a different master.
   - He is servile, not defiant as he was before.
   - All the characters are drunk and the scene is broadly comic.
   - Caliban unexpectedly speaks in verse and describes the island poetically.
   - Perhaps this shows what he could have been if Prospero had not enslaved him – or perhaps his eloquence is the result of the education Prospero gave him.
   - Caliban sings about his freedom. His joy might be genuine, but he is not actually free.
   - The play is influenced by the colonisation of places like America happening at the time, with settlers enslaving indigenous peoples.
   - Caliban and Ariel are sometimes seen as two different kinds of slave.
   - Prospero also enslaves Ferdinand to test his love.
   - In a sense, all the characters are imprisoned on the island and most are freed at the end.

4. **Much Ado About Nothing**
   - Don John is Don Pedro's brother but, as a bastard, is an outsider with no power.
   - He claims that he is honest and will not pretend to gain favour.
   - This is the first time we see him – he is talking to his confidant, Conrad, so we can take what he says as the truth.
   - Conrad urges him to co-operate now he has been defeated by Don Pedro.
   - They both use natural imagery – Conrad talks about a 'harvest' but Don John of being 'a canker in a hedge'.
   - We will see later the use he makes of his discontent as he plots against Claudio and Hero.
   - His actions provide the plot of the play, both by causing Claudio to reject Hero and, indirectly, bringing Beatrice and Benedick together.
   - His presence casts a shadow over the play. He stands apart from the happiness of the others at the end.
   - He can be seen as a 'malcontent', an unhappy character at odds with the world, common in plays of the time.

5. **The Merchant of Venice**
   - Portia is in control, telling Bassanio what she wants.
   - However, she is controlled by the will of her dead father.
   - She is obedient to her father's wishes, not wanting to be 'forsworn'.
   - Making a good marriage is important to her as well as to her father, but she wants to marry the man she loves.
   - She speaks openly of her love for Bassanio while stating that 'a maiden hath no tongue but thought', meaning she has no real power.
   - Jessica, like Portia, is controlled by her father but she asserts her independence by eloping.
   - Portia and Nerissa disguise themselves as men, which is necessary if Portia is to be taken seriously.
   - All three women express themselves openly and behave independently, following their hearts.

6. **Julius Caesar**
   - Brutus's suicide would be seen as honourable by Romans.
   - Antony makes a distinction between Brutus and the others – 'only he' had 'honest' motives.
   - Brutus is seen as a good politician, interested in 'common good to all'.
   - He is also praised as a man – he was 'gentle' and he lacked the vice of envy.
   - Antony uses rhetoric to proclaim Brutus's worth, imagining nature itself praising him.
   - Octavius echoes Antony's sentiments, wanting him treated 'according to his virtue'.
   - Their sentiments are especially important because they were his enemies.
   - In his conversations with Cassius, Brutus is shown as the idealist, an honourable man.
   - He is important to the conspiracy because of his reputation.
   - He is a brave soldier and leader who inspires love and loyalty.

Section B: The 19th-Century Novel

See mark scheme on page 66 for Section A. This question does not carry additional marks for AO4.

Your answers could include some of the following points.

7. **The Strange Case of Dr Jekyll and Mr Hyde**
   - The description of the scene at twilight creates a sad, gentle mood.
   - Jekyll is compared to a 'disconsolate prisoner', making him seem like a victim.
   - Jekyll's words about being 'low' and it 'will not last long' suggest an illness he is not in control of.
   - Jekyll is polite and pleasant when speaking to the visitors.
   - The sudden change in his look is frightening and the 'terror and despair' is like the reaction of a victim.
   - Jekyll is discussed by Utterson and Lanyon as someone who used to be a good, reasonable man but has become strange.
   - His friends are inclined to see him as a victim of Hyde and want to help him.
   - Dr Lanyon's narrative reveals the full horror of what Jekyll has become and his 'moral turpitude'.
   - Jekyll's own narrative gives us insight into his motives and his feelings about what he has done, making him sympathetic again.

8. **A Christmas Carol**
   - The Cratchits show their love for Tim and for each other after the 'death' of Tiny Tim.
   - Mrs Cratchit is anxious about Bob, not thinking of herself.
   - Bob tries to be positive, speaking of the 'green place' where Tim is to be buried, but breaks down.
   - Contrast between reactions to Scrooge's death and Tiny Tim's.

- The reaction of Scrooge's nephew contrasts with how Scrooge treats people including the Cratchits.
- The Cratchits represent decent hard-working people who find it hard to get by.
- They are the model of a loving, cheerful family, and show the true spirit of Christmas.
- Scrooge's treatment of Bob shows him to be a bad employer, in contrast with his old boss Fezziwig.
- Scrooge learns from watching the Cratchits at home. Their home life is the opposite of his.
- Sending the turkey to the Cratchits shows how much Scrooge has changed.

9. *Great Expectations*
- The setting in the graveyard makes Magwitch's first appearance terrifying and memorable.
- He is described as an intimidating figure and is clearly an escaped convict, but his cold and hunger might make him sympathetic.
- His speech, rough both in content and style, is in stark contrast to Pip's.
- Although frightening to young Pip, there is a comic element to the character brought out by the adult narrator.
- His physical strength is emphasised.
- He is absent for most of the novel and not even mentioned so that his reappearance comes as a surprise.
- Pip's reaction to discovering he is his benefactor puts Pip in an unsympathetic light – he mentions his 'abhorrence'.
- In contrast to Pip and his 'expectations', Magwitch succeeds and makes money through hard work.
- Magwitch tells his own story, making him sympathetic and correcting a lot of Pip's misunderstandings.
- The fact that he could turn Pip into a gentleman – and that he is Estella's father – questions the idea of social class and privilege.
- He is like a father to Pip and Pip comes to see that he is a 'better man'.

10. *Jane Eyre*
- Jane is included in the party but sits apart, listening and not making a contribution.
- She slips out by a side door, wanting to be as unobtrusive as possible.
- Rochester seems concerned about her but questions her abruptly.
- He also gives her orders: 'Return to the drawing-room'.
- She is conscious of not having the 'freedom' to speak to him as an equal.
- She is from an upper or upper-middle class background but is impoverished and has to earn a living.
- Her position means that she can mix with (and observe) servants as well as employers and their friends.
- She does not like the affectations of people like the snobbish Ingrams.
- Her judgments are not based on class – she can praise or condemn people regardless of their background.
- Rochester does not care about her class or background.
- Ultimately, though, she returns to her 'proper' position in life, getting an inheritance as well as a 'good' marriage.

11. *Frankenstein*
- Frankenstein compares his enthusiasm to a 'hurricane' and there is a sense of violent haste about the account.
- He admits that pride and ambition motivate him.
- There is a sense of the virtue of pursuing knowledge, bringing 'a torrent of light into our dark world'.
- However, his language betrays a desire to 'play God' by becoming a 'creator'.
- His description of the 'horrors' of his work, digging up bones, etc., conveys a sense of revulsion at odds with his ideas about doing something noble.
- This is seen as 'profane', against religion and God, in desecrating holy ground.
- After giving the creature life, Frankenstein is instantly repelled and rejects his creation.
- He makes no attempt to care for or educate the creature, which therefore has to learn from its experience.

- He becomes afraid of the creature and remorseful about his actions.
- He is punished for his act of creation by the deeds of the creature and his own misery.

12. *Pride and Prejudice*
- Austen describes Mr Collins's reaction ironically by using the kind of hyperbolic vocabulary he might have used – 'triumph', 'grandeur'.
- His 'triumph' depends on others ('his wondering visitors') being as snobbish.
- Sir William responds in the same way, showing off about his own 'situation in life', to assert his superiority to Mr Collins.
- Mr Collins assumes others will be as impressed as he is and keen that the experience does not 'overpower' them – the implication being that he hopes it does.
- His advice to Elizabeth about her dress is comic because of its inappropriateness – as a man he would not be expected to discuss such things with ladies.
- Snobbery is shown by his concern with superficial things like how people dress and how many rooms they have.
- What he says about Lady Catherine and the 'distinction of rank' proves to be true, showing that she is a snob.
- Darcy is also a snob, though not as obviously as his aunt. This is shown in his behaviour at the Meryton ball.
- Jane's romance with Bingley shows the snobbishness of his sisters and the damaging effect it can have.
- Elizabeth might also be a bit of a snob. Consider her feelings about her family's behaviour at Netherfield Park.

13. *The Sign of Four*
- Watson is excited about showing the treasure to Miss Morston and proud of being allowed to bring it.
- He may see the treasure as proof of his love for her.
- She has 'no eagerness in her voice', surprising us by her apparent 'indifference' to the treasure.
- Tension and expectation are built by the description of the box and the difficulty of opening it.
- The treasure box is exotic and incongruous in Mrs Forrester's house, the use of Mrs Forrester's poker adding some humour.
- As soon as he sees the box is empty, he feels the same, showing their mutual love.
- Finding the treasure seemed to be the point of the adventure but finding the truth is more important.
- The pursuit of it has placed Holmes, Watson and others in 'horrible peril'.
- It is the motive for the killing of Jonathan Sholto and the reason for the death of Morston.
- The story of Jonathan Small shows that the Agra treasure – or rather the desire of people to possess it – has always caused unhappiness and death.

Page 50 English Literature Paper 2 – Modern Texts and Poetry

Section A: Modern Prose or Drama
See mark scheme on page 66 for English Literature Paper 1.
This question carries **[30]** marks plus **[4]** marks for AO4 to a maximum of **[34]**.
Your answers could include some of the following points.

1. *An Inspector Calls*
- Priestley presents a very unequal society – we see the rich middle-class Birlings and hear about Eva Smith.
- Eva experiences many problems, such as losing her job and getting pregnant.
- At the time the play is set, there is little help for her.
- Priestley wrote the play in the 1940s when there was a lot of discussion about the welfare state.
- Eva could be several different girls with different problems. Eva is a device for bringing them to our attention.
- Daisy Renton, the girl Gerald was involved with, could be the same girl as Eva or she could be a different person, used to show how little the Birlings value people of her class.
- Her problems can be seen in terms of socialism and/or feminism. Are they the result of her class or her gender?

- The central message is about taking responsibility for each other.

2.
- The Inspector takes charge and commands respect.
- He is an 'outsider' and does not belong to the world the Birlings move in.
- He acts like a detective in that he is investigating something and asking a lot of questions.
- He is not really investigating a crime but is looking into the reasons for Eva's act.
- He apportions blame and judges the other characters.
- He moralises about society and warns of the consequences of acting like the Birlings.
- His name, Goole, is pronounced the same as 'ghoul'. Is he a ghost from the future?
- He has come from the 1940s, the time the play was written, to examine an earlier time.
- He may be warning the audience not to return to the society of 1912.
- He can be seen as the voice of the writer.

3. **Blood Brothers**
- Mrs Johnstone makes a choice to give away (or sell) her child.
- Her choice may be justified by her economic circumstances.
- There is a sense that tragedy is inevitable, expressed by the narrator.
- Is this because of what she has done or because of class and poverty?
- Mickey is seen as the victim of social inequality.
- However, he makes bad choices throughout the play.
- The writer's (and audience's) sympathies seem to be entirely with Mrs Johnstone and Mickey.
- The two boys are not different in nature – their differences are the result of upbringing.

4.
- Linda stands up for Mickey to his brother and the other older children.
- She is one of the gang, equal to the boys in their games.
- She is protective and caring towards Mickey.
- The conversation about dying prefigures the end of the play, as does Sammy's gun.
- She is pragmatic in a comic, childish way: 'if y'dead, there's no school'.
- Here, Mickey introduces Linda to Edward for the first time. Their relationship will be crucial.
- In the park, Linda proves better than the boys at shooting: is Russell making a feminist point?
- She is outgoing and witty, and she helps to create a lighter atmosphere as she and the boys have fun together.
- She is in love with Mickey but, as his wife, is frustrated in her attempts to help him.
- She turns to Edward for help, unwittingly bringing the tragedy closer.

5. **The History Boys**
- The Headmaster sees education as a competition – the boys' success reflects on the school.
- He is not an academic high-flyer and is in awe of Oxford and Cambridge.
- He does not give away what he really thinks about issues such as Hector's 'fiddling'.
- He has a distant relationship with the teachers and pupils. Teachers call him 'Headmaster'.
- He uses the teachers and manipulates them, especially Irwin against Hector.
- In turn he is manipulated and controlled by Dakin.
- His public language is formal and authoritative (as in his last speech) while in private it is coarse.
- He could be seen as being interested in self-preservation and taking credit for others' efforts.

6.
- Mrs Lintott says Posner wants to know if Irwin has 'ceased to be a teacher and become a friend', implying you cannot be both.
- Posner is looking for personal advice, which could be seen as part of a teacher's job.

- Irwin seeks to discover more about Hector's relationship with the boys. This could be seen as crossing a professional line or as showing concern about Hector crossing lines.
- Posner notices Irwin's interest in Dakin. Dakin takes advantage of this attraction and treats Irwin as a friend.
- Hector blurs the lines between teacher/pupil relationships and friendship. Even without the 'groping', he could be seen as over-friendly.
- It could be said that a 'friendly' relationship with pupils is helpful in teaching but that is not the same as becoming friends.
- At times, the friendship between staff and pupils can seem fun and positive but it can also be harmful and manipulative (on both sides).

7. **DNA**
- All the characters are teenagers. We are in their world.
- The 'killing' of Adam is shocking and shows what they are capable of.
- Their reaction, blaming the postman, might be more shocking.
- They are part of a gang/friendship group but also belong to smaller groups.
- The interaction between them and the way they talk is typically 'teenage' – normal in spite of the abnormality of their actions.
- Their relationships with adults are not shown, only reported by them, but seem distant.
- They are distinct characters with different reactions, so not just stereotypical teenagers.
- They are dominated by strong characters and the demands of the group.

8.
- Cathy is not seen as the leader at first but takes over later in the play.
- She wants to be popular.
- It is she who gets the DNA from the postman.
- She finds the events after Adam's disappearance exciting.
- She does not feel guilty, seeming to have no sense of right and wrong.
- She enjoys the attention of the media and other people.
- She thinks about gaining materially from the situation.
- She takes control of the group and then the whole school.
- She is power-hungry, ruthless and bullying as leader.

9. **The Curious Incident of the Dog in the Night-Time**
- He finds people confusing. Christopher articulates his perspective on the world.
- He speaks differently from other characters, saying what he thinks without embellishment.
- Other characters are conscious of treating him differently, e.g. not touching him.
- His relationship with Siobhan marks him out as 'officially' different as in having special needs.
- His parents demonstrate how his 'difference' affects those close to him.
- His thoughts are presented through Siobhan reading his notes.
- The way he experiences life is presented theatrically, e.g. by the voices when he arrives at the station.

10.
- Christopher is concerned by the fact that he has been accused of killing Wellington.
- He like facts and is not willing to let this go – he needs to know the truth.
- He applies his own logic to the case, based on dogs being as important as people.
- Ed's reaction suggests to the audience (but not to literal-minded Christopher) that he is hiding something.
- Christopher's investigation will lead him to uncover the truth about other things, like his parents' marriage.
- He becomes more independent, taking the initiative and facing his fears, e.g. on the train.
- Other characters may begin to value him more, but does he value them more?
- He himself attributes his increased confidence and success to the incident, referring to how he went to London on his own.

- We are left wondering how much he can achieve.
- How much has he changed? And if he has not changed, does it matter?

11. *A Taste of Honey*
- The play's main characters are Jo and Helen, the men being incidental characters.
- Jo's relationships with men may be a reaction to her mother's attitudes.
- Helen uses men for money and sex. She depends on them but does not respect them.
- Jo's relationship with the Boy is romantic but brief.
- He lets her down, shattering her dreams.
- The Boy and Geof are outsiders (like Jo), one because of race and the other because of sexuality.
- Peter is unpleasant and overbearing.
- All the men leave Jo in the end, leaving her with Helen and facing an independent but uncertain future.

12.
- Jo shows immaturity and lack of understanding of what motherhood will mean.
- Her attitude might be a way of avoiding her true feelings.
- She does not say she wants to be a mother but refuses to consider abortion.
- She says she does not know much about love – will she be able to love the baby?
- Geof, not knowing her, assumes Helen will care because she is Jo's mother.
- Later Jo panics and says, 'I don't want to be a mother'.
- Geof tries to help her but she reacts by joking and flirting, trying to avoid the subject of motherhood.
- Helen's idea of being a mother is unconventional.
- She is selfish and shows little concern for Jo.
- She becomes sentimental about the baby but focuses on material things like the cot.
- Their love–hate relationship is the central one in both their lives.

13. *Lord of the Flies*
- Simon is the opposite of Jack. He is inherently good.
- He is gentle, and kind to the 'little 'uns'.
- He has the same sort of background as the other boys but for him ideas about morality and civilisation are not superficial.
- He understands what the 'beast' means.
- His hallucinations are almost mystical and holy.
- His murder represents the ultimate triumph of evil and savagery.
- He can be seen as a sacrificial victim, perhaps like Jesus.

14.
- Being British is a shorthand for being civilised.
- The boys' ideas of correct behaviour are entwined with ideas about being British, learned at home and at public school.
- The officer talks about British boys putting on a 'better show'.
- Being British means coping with adversity.
- At the time the novel was written, Britain's place in the world was changing, the days of Empire coming to an end.
- The sense of 'Britishness' alluded to by the officer is a male upper-class concept.
- The novel is influenced by the kind of boys' adventure stories popular in the nineteenth and early twentieth centuries, in which British boys overcame danger and adversity.
- Britain is associated with colonialism – the events of the novel undermine the idea of colonialism.
- Golding implicitly criticises all nation states, not just Britain, and their involvement in wars.

15. *Telling Tales*
- In 'Korea', the narrator at first seems to have a good relationship with his father as they go fishing together.
- They cooperate and work well together.
- Fishing is part of a disappearing way of life, reflecting the change that will come for the family.
- When he overhears his father talking about Korea, the boy realises how his father feels towards him.

- The older generation seem to think more of themselves and money than of their children.
- Compare with the distance between father and son in 'A Family Supper'.
- Compare with the discovery of cruelty and violence in the older generation in 'The Darkness Out There'.
- Compare the two narrators and their reactions in 'Korea' and 'Chemistry'.

16.
- At the beginning of 'The Darkness Out There', stories about crashed planes and girls being attacked are just rumours to Sandra, not reality.
- Her walk to the cottage in the woods is reminiscent of a fairy tale.
- Mrs Rutter's story reveals the reality of war and death.
- The young people are shocked at how Mrs Rutter and her sister behaved.
- Sandra sees Kerry differently because of his angry reaction: 'older' and 'larger'.
- She feels that her life is changed and sees the 'darkness out there'.
- Compare with the way in which the narrator learns about death and growing up in 'Chemistry'.
- Compare with the change in the narrator's feelings about his father in 'Korea'.
- Compare the change to Elizabeth's life in 'The Odour of Chrysanthemums'.

17. *Animal Farm*
- Old Major is 'wise' and respected by the other animals, so his ideas are listened to.
- He makes a logical and persuasive case against Man. He sounds reasonable.
- His 'dream' gives an almost mystical power to his ideas.
- Although he talks about rebellion, he does not make any practical plans for it and says it might not come for a long time.
- He is the equivalent of Vladimir Lenin, whose ideas shaped communism.
- He dies before the rebellion so we cannot know whether he would have remained an idealist.
- It is up to others to put his ideas into practice and interpret them.
- After the rebellion, his ideas are changed and his followers corrupted.
- This reflects the history of the USSR and other regimes based on egalitarian ideals.

18.
- Old Major blames humans for all the animals' problems.
- He states that 'we must not come to resemble them' and lists things that animals must never do.
- Even when they are putting up the commandments, the pigs give instructions to the other animals.
- The pigs learn human skills and take privileges for themselves.
- Squealer stops opposition by threatening the return of humans.
- They breed dogs to keep order; the dogs follow Napoleon as they did Mr Jones.
- The pigs start dealing with humans, using money and sleeping at the farmhouse, but have an answer for every criticism.
- The other animals change from being willing comrades and supporters to being confused and questioning, but they continue to obey the pigs.
- The pigs eventually rule by terror and are more cruel than humans.
- At the end, the pigs are indistinguishable from men, their transformation complete.
- These changes reflect the changes in the behaviour of leaders in communist and other populist regimes.

19. *Never Let Me Go*
- Kathy is a first-person narrator and we see everything through her eyes.
- She is a naïve narrator as she does not understand a lot of what is happening.

- Her tone is chatty, and she shares her feelings and reactions openly.
- She is proud of her success as a 'carer', working within the system.
- She is not quick to question but she listens to Tommy.
- Her naïvety and lack of understanding mean that we discover things gradually with her.
- She forms strong emotional relationships, demonstrating her humanity.

20.
- Ruth voices her feelings about being a clone, which no-one else has articulated.
- The word 'clone' is rarely used in the novel and for a long time the reader might not realise the characters are clones.
- Ruth feels that the others are living a fantasy, trying to make themselves feel better.
- She associates clones with 'trash' – they are even less than the worst humans.
- In spite of the clones knowing that they are different, they have human emotions and human relationships.
- Kathy feels that their 'human' behaviour is learned, with her friends imitating relationships and behaviour they see on television.
- At the end, her feelings are no different from the feelings of any human.
- We see everything through a clone's eyes, leading us to wonder what the difference is between clones and humans.
- We might ask whether it will be possible to create clones in this way and, if so, will they feel and think like humans?

21. *Anita and Me*
- Syal describes Indian dress and food in great detail.
- The narrator is very aware of her 'different' culture.
- The visits of the aunts, uncles and Nanima bring Indian culture to Tollington.
- Meena is not always happy about being different and is drawn to the culture of Tollington.
- Religion is part of the culture but it is not as important to Meena's parents as to others.
- The stories told by her family give Meena a sense of culture, tradition and history.
- At the end, when they move, she embraces Indian culture and her ethnic identity more fully.

22.
- The house is described as old-fashioned and uncomfortable.
- Meena's father gets 'sick of it' and its distance from work.
- Tollington's situation in the countryside appeals to Meena's mother.
- She likes it because it reminds her of home in the Punjab.
- She is seen as unusual and odd by other Indians who want modern houses nearer the city.
- Tollington itself is a poor, run-down village; part of its appeal to the young Meena is its size and the sense of community.
- The family is conscious of being the only Indian family and therefore the object of curiosity and prejudice.
- They are also middle class and better educated than most of their neighbours and they sometimes look down on them.
- As Meena gets older, she becomes more aware of racism and the differences between her and other Tollington residents.

23. *Pigeon English*
- The novel opens with a murder and Harrison becomes obsessed with 'the dead boy'.
- He witnesses the violent attack on Mr Frimpong and is drawn into a world of violent gangs.
- At first he is excited by violence but he comes to understand the reality of it.
- There is violence in school and among teenagers outside school.
- Aunty Sonia has harmed herself to stay in the country.
- Miquita suffers violence from her boyfriend.

- It is a world of gangs, knives and guns – even the police on the tube have guns.
- The climax, when Harrison is murdered, seems inevitable.

24.
- Mamma is a dominant character in Harrison's life.
- She is seen as hard-working and caring, perhaps a stereotypical African mother.
- Aunty Sonia is entertaining and fascinating but her self-harm is disturbing.
- Lydia is a stereotypical older sister, fighting with Harrison and bossing him around.
- Harrison's crush on Poppy gives some relief from the violence.
- Women, such as Miquita and Aunty Sonia, are seen as victims of violence.
- Although they are portrayed as strong personalities, they are largely ineffective.
- The gangs depicted are all male and the violence is mostly done by males.
- Adult males, if not violent or criminal, do not feature much in Harrison's life.

Section B: Poetry

For both questions 25 and 26, look at the mark scheme below, decide which description is closest to your answer and then decide which mark to give yourself up to a maximum of **[30]**.

Marks	Skills
26–30	<ul><li>You have compared texts in an exploratory and critical way.</li><li>You have used precise, appropriate references to support your interpretation.</li><li>You have analysed the writers' methods using subject terminology appropriately.</li><li>You have explored the effects of the writers' methods.</li><li>You have explored links between text and ideas/context.</li></ul>
21–25	<ul><li>You have made thoughtful, developed comparisons.</li><li>You have used appropriate references to support your interpretation.</li><li>You have examined the writers' methods using subject terminology appropriately.</li><li>You have examined the effects of the writers' methods.</li><li>You have thoughtfully considered links between text and ideas/context.</li></ul>
16–20	<ul><li>You have made clear comparisons.</li><li>You have used references effectively to support your explanation.</li><li>You have explained the writers' methods using relevant subject terminology.</li><li>You have understood the effects of the writers' methods.</li><li>You have clearly considered links between text and ideas/context.</li></ul>

25. Your answer might include comparisons such as:
- Relationship with a parent – 'Follower', 'Eden Rock', 'Walking Away', 'Mother, any distance.'
- Memories/nostalgia – 'Follower', 'Eden Rock', 'Walking Away', 'Neutral Tones', When We Two Parted'.
- A sense of place – 'Eden Rock', 'Follower', 'Letter from Yorkshire'.
- References to popular culture, etc. to give a sense of period – 'Eden Rock', 'Walking Away'.
- Direct address to the poem's subject – 'Winter Swans', Sonnet 29, 'When We Two Parted', 'Neutral Tones', 'Love's Philosophy', 'Letters from Yorkshire', 'Walking Away'.
- Colloquial language – 'Singh Song!'.
- Division into stanzas of equal length – 'Neutral Tones', Eden Rock', 'Love's Philosophy, 'When We Two Parted'.
- Use of half-rhyme – 'Follower', 'Winter Swans'.

26. Your answer might include comparisons such as:
- Experience of a battle/war – 'The Charge of the Light Brigade', 'Exposure', 'Bayonet Charge'.
- First-person account of a life-changing experience – 'The Prelude', 'Exposure'.
- Persona adopted by the poet – 'My Last Duchess'.
- Poem based on reports/research (not personal experience) – 'The Charge of the Light Brigade', 'Bayonet Charge', 'War Photographer', contrast 'Exposure'.
- Colloquial language – 'Exposure'.
- Individual shaped/haunted by memory – 'War Photographer', 'The Emigrée', 'The Prelude'.
- Violent imagery and diction – 'Exposure', 'Bayonet Charge', 'War Photographer'.
- Use of present tense – 'Exposure', contrast 'The Charge of the Light Brigade' and 'Bayonet Charge'.
- Structure – stanzas of equal length, varied line length. Change at end.
- No regular metre of rhyme scheme but some rhyme and half-rhyme – 'Exposure', 'Storm on the Island'.

Section C: Unseen Poetry

27-1. Look at the mark scheme below, decide which description is closest to your answer and then decide which mark to give yourself up to a maximum of **[24]**.

Marks	Skills
21–24	• You have explored the text critically. • You have used precise references to support your interpretation. • You have analysed the writer's methods using appropriate subject terminology. • You have explored the effects of the writer's methods on the reader.
17–20	• You have responded thoughtfully to the text. • You have used appropriate references to support your interpretation. • You have examined the writer's methods using subject terminology effectively. • You have examined the effects of the writer's methods on the reader.
13–16	• You have responded clearly to the text. • You have used references effectively to support your interpretation. • You have explained the writer's methods using relevant subject terminology. • You have understood the effects of the writer's methods on the reader.

Your answer might include comments on:
- Comparison of frost to a ghost sets the mood and makes us think of death.
- Depressing mood continues with language like 'dregs', 'desolate' and 'weakening'.
- Landscape and weather reflects the poet's mood – pathetic fallacy.
- In the second stanza, Hardy places himself in the landscape.
- He associates the landscape with passing time, as the century (nineteenth) comes to an end.

- He uses an extended metaphor of a corpse, continuing the morbid theme.
- The use of alliteration of hard 'c' gives a sharp, uncomfortable tone.
- There is a sudden change ('At once') with the sound of the thrush.
- Contrast of the 'joy' of the thrush with the death-like landscape.
- Religious imagery in 'evensong', 'soul' and 'carolings'.
- The age and weakness of the thrush makes his singing more extraordinary.
- Hardy sees the thrush as making an active choice to 'fling his soul'.
- The poet is unaware of the 'blessed Hope' but the thrush's song shows him the possibility of hope.

27-2. Look at the mark scheme below, decide which description is closest to your answer and then decide which mark to give yourself up to a maximum of **[8]**.

Marks	Skills
7–8	• You have explored comparisons of the writers' use of language, structure and form. • You have used appropriate subject terminology. • You have convincingly compared the effects of the writers' methods on the reader.
5–6	• You have thoughtfully compared the writers' use of language, structure and/or form. • You have used effective subject terminology. • You have clearly compared the effects of the writers' methods on the reader.

Your answer might include comments on:
- In both of them, the poet is alone in the landscape.
- The landscape and weather are harsh in both, reflecting the poets' moods.
- In 'The Darkling Thrush' the poet's mood is changed but in 'Spellbound' it remains the same.
- Brontë does not say what the 'tyrant spell' is, whether it is from nature or her own feelings. Similarly, Hardy does not explain his mood.
- Hardy writes about an incident in the past – Brontë writes in the present tense.
- Brontë's natural imagery is literal and simple, while Hardy uses an elaborate extended metaphor in the second stanza, as well as a simile in the first stanza.
- Brontë uses repetition and a refrain to give a sense of her situation.
- At first Brontë seems powerless but the last line suggests she is choosing to be where she is ('I will not').
- While the weather depresses Hardy and his mood is rescued by the thrush, Brontë seems to rejoice in the 'dreary' night.
- Both poems are regular in form and structure.

Acknowledgements

The author and publisher are grateful to the copyright holders for permission to use quoted materials and images.

Every effort has been made to trace copyright holders and obtain their permission for the use of copyright material. The author and publisher will gladly receive information enabling them to rectify any error or omission in subsequent editions. All facts are correct at time of going to press.

P30 *Checking Out Me History* copyright © John Agard 1996 reproduced by kind permission of John Agard c/o Caroline Sheldon Literary Agency Ltd. P30, P55 'Before You Were Mine' from *Mean Time* by Carol Ann Duffy. Published by Picador. Copyright © Carol Ann Duffy. Reproduced by permission of the author c/o Rogers, Coleridge & White Ltd.,

20 Powis Mews, London W11 1JN. P30 *Storm on the Island* from 'Death of a Naturalist' by Seamus Heaney (Faber and Faber Ltd). P56 'Remains' by Simon Armitage. Copyright © Simon Armitage.

Published by Collins
An imprint of HarperCollins*Publishers* Ltd
1 London Bridge Street, London, SE1 9GF

HarperCollins*Publishers* Macken House, 39/40 Mayor Street Upper, Dublin 1, DO1 C9W8, Ireland

© HarperCollins*Publishers* Limited 2022

ISBN 9780008535049

First published 2015
This edition published 2022

10 9 8 7 6 5 4 3 2

British Library Cataloguing in Publication Data.

A CIP record of this book is available from the British Library.

Author: Paul Burns
Cover Design: Kevin Robbins and Sarah Duxbury
Inside Concept Design: Sarah Duxbury and Paul Oates
Text Design and Layout: Jouve India Private limited
Printed by Ashford Colour Press Ltd